I0011725

TOR AND DEEP WEB

Master Your Online Privacy,
Darknet, NSA, Spying,
Bitcoin, Mining, Ethereum,
Blockchain,

Hacking, and more!

2 Books in 1

Ryan Knight

Table of Contents

TOR BLUEPRINT

NAVIGATING THE DARKNET AND DEEP WEB, KALI LINUX, HACKING ETHICALLY, AND FORTIFYING YOUR DIGITAL FORTRESS

INTRODUCTION: UNVEILING THE TOR BLUEPRINT

Embarking on a journey into the intricate realms of cybersecurity, our exploration begins with a profound introduction that sets the stage for a comprehensive understanding of TOR, Kali Linux, ethical hacking, and the critical importance of digital fortification. In this opening chapter, we delve into the intricacies of each component, laying the groundwork for a holistic exploration that transcends the superficial layers of digital security.

TOR

Our first point of focus is TOR, the renowned acronym for The Onion Router, a privacy-focused network that enables users to navigate the digital landscape with a heightened level of anonymity. As we set the stage, it's imperative to unveil the veil of anonymity that TOR provides. We will explore the architecture of TOR, understanding the layers of encryption that make up its distinctive onion structure. By comprehending the intricacies of TOR, readers will gain insights into the mechanisms that empower them to traverse the digital landscape incognito.

The introductory chapter will also guide readers through the process of setting up and utilizing TOR for secure browsing.

We aim not only to explain the theoretical aspects but also to provide practical steps, ensuring readers can apply their newfound knowledge in real-world scenarios. TOR becomes not just a theoretical concept but a tangible tool in the readers' hands as they venture further into the realms of digital security.

Kali Linux: The Arsenal for Cybersecurity Warriors

As we transition within the opening chapter, the spotlight turns to Kali Linux, a potent operating system designed specifically for penetration testing and ethical hacking. Setting the stage for a deep dive into Kali Linux involves unraveling its essentials. This includes an exploration of the myriad tools at the disposal of cybersecurity warriors, each meticulously crafted to identify vulnerabilities, assess security, and fortify digital environments.

We aim to make Kali Linux accessible, breaking down complex tools into digestible components. The goal is not just to introduce Kali Linux but to empower readers with a practical understanding of how to leverage its tools. From reconnaissance to exploitation and post-exploitation, readers will gain proficiency in utilizing Kali Linux as a powerful ally in their quest for digital security.

Ethical Hacking: The Responsible Approach

As the narrative unfolds, ethical hacking emerges as a central theme. In the context of setting the stage, it is crucial to define ethical hacking and underline its pivotal role in fortifying digital systems. The chapter will delve into the nuances of ethical hacking, distinguishing it from malicious activities and emphasizing its ethical and legal foundations.

Readers will be introduced to ethical hacking methodologies, tools, and best practices. The goal is not only to equip them with the technical skills necessary for ethical hacking but also to cultivate a mindset that prioritizes responsible and lawful conduct in the realm of cybersecurity. Ethical hacking becomes a means of proactively identifying vulnerabilities, ensuring that readers approach the digital landscape with a sense of responsibility and integrity.

Digital Fortification: Beyond the Basics

With TOR, Kali Linux, and ethical hacking as foundational pillars, the stage is set for an exploration of digital fortification. This extends beyond the basics of securing passwords and employing encryption. The chapter will guide readers through advanced security strategies, offering a comprehensive guide to fortifying digital assets against an evolving landscape of cyber threats.

We delve into the intricacies of penetration testing as a proactive measure. Readers will not only understand the concept of penetration testing but will be provided with practical examples and exercises to apply these techniques. The objective is to go beyond theoretical discussions, ensuring that readers are capable of implementing these strategies in real-world scenarios.

Navigating Legal and Moral Boundaries

As we approach the conclusion of the introductory chapter, ethical considerations take center stage once again. Navigating legal and moral boundaries in the world of ethical hacking becomes a crucial aspect of digital security. The chapter will explore the importance of ethical conduct, providing guidance on navigating the legal landscape and upholding moral standards in the pursuit of cybersecurity.

The goal is to instill in readers a sense of responsibility, emphasizing that ethical hacking is not a carte blanche for unrestricted exploration but a disciplined and principled approach to securing digital environments. By addressing the ethical dimensions of cybersecurity, the stage is set for a journey that is not only technically proficient but also ethically grounded.

A Call to Craft Your Digital Legacy

As we continue this introductory chapter, the narrative circles back to the overarching theme of crafting a digital legacy. Summarizing key takeaways, readers are inspired to apply their newfound knowledge to create a secure and ethical digital presence. The stage is set not only for technical proficiency but for a holistic approach to digital security that transcends the immediate challenges and extends into the long-term responsibility of safeguarding one's digital legacy.

In this extensive exploration, the introductory chapter serves as a compass, guiding readers through the multifaceted landscape of TOR, Kali Linux, ethical hacking, and digital fortification. It lays the foundation for a journey that is both technically enriching and ethically enlightening, setting the tone for what promises to be a transformative exploration into the realms of cybersecurity.

Establishing the book's commitment to providing a practical guide for readers of varying skill levels.

Establishing the book's commitment to providing a practical guide for readers of varying skill levels is not just a matter of stating intentions but requires a careful articulation of the methodologies and approaches that will be employed throughout the book. In this section, we delve into the core principles that underscore this commitment, ensuring that readers, regardless of their expertise, find valuable insights and actionable steps to enhance their understanding of TOR, Kali Linux, ethical hacking, and digital fortification.

Understanding the Audience: A Spectrum of Skill Levels

The first step in establishing our commitment to practical guidance is acknowledging the diverse audience that the book aims to serve. Recognizing that readers may span a spectrum of skill levels, from beginners with limited technical knowledge to seasoned cybersecurity professionals, is crucial. The commitment lies in tailoring the content to meet the unique needs and expectations of each reader, creating a resource that is inclusive and accessible.

Layered Learning: A Gradual Unveiling of Complexity

In the commitment to providing practical guidance, the book adopts a layered learning approach. Each concept, whether it be TOR, Kali Linux, ethical hacking, or digital fortification, is presented in a way that allows for a gradual understanding of complexity. The book begins with foundational principles, ensuring that even readers with minimal background knowledge can grasp the essential concepts. As the chapters progress, layers of complexity are added, offering a scaffolded learning experience that builds upon the reader's understanding.

Hands-On Application: Bridging Theory and Practice

A crucial aspect of providing a practical guide is the integration of hands-on application. The book doesn't merely present theoretical concepts; it encourages readers to actively apply what they learn. Whether it's setting up TOR for the first time, navigating the deep web, or experimenting with ethical hacking tools in Kali Linux, readers are guided through practical exercises. This approach ensures that theoretical knowledge transforms into tangible skills, empowering readers to implement what they've learned in real-world scenarios.

Case Studies and Scenarios: Real-World Relevance

To reinforce the commitment to practicality, the book incorporates real-world case studies and scenarios. By examining actual examples of cybersecurity challenges and solutions, readers gain insights into the practical applications of the concepts discussed. Whether it's a case study illustrating the impact of a security breach or a scenario demonstrating the effectiveness of ethical hacking in a corporate setting, these real-world examples enhance the relevance of the content and its applicability in professional contexts.

Adaptability: Tailoring Content to Reader Progression

Understanding that readers progress at different rates, the book is structured to accommodate varying paces of learning. Each chapter builds on the previous one, but the content is designed to be adaptable. Readers can choose to delve deeper into advanced topics or focus on mastering the fundamentals, depending on their comfort level and goals. This adaptability ensures that the book remains a relevant and valuable resource throughout different stages of the reader's learning journey.

Interactive Elements: Engaging the Reader

The commitment to practical guidance extends to the incorporation of interactive elements within the book. This includes quizzes, exercises, and interactive demonstrations that actively engage the reader. Interactive elements serve not only to reinforce learning but also to make the educational experience dynamic and enjoyable. The book becomes more than just a static source of information; it transforms into an interactive learning platform that accommodates various learning styles.

Expert Insights: Balancing Depth and Accessibility

Recognizing the varying skill levels among readers, the book strikes a balance between depth and accessibility. Expert insights are woven into the narrative, providing in-depth explanations and advanced techniques for readers with a higher proficiency in cybersecurity. Simultaneously, the content is presented in a clear and accessible manner for beginners, ensuring that the book remains an effective resource for a broad readership.

Continuous Support: A Learning Journey, Not a Destination

The commitment to providing a practical guide extends beyond the pages of the book. Recognizing that cybersecurity is a dynamic field with ever-evolving challenges, the book encourages readers to embark on a continuous learning journey. Resources for further exploration, online communities, and updates from the author ensure that readers have ongoing support in their quest for knowledge and skill development.

Empowering Readers with Practical Proficiency

In conclusion, establishing the book's commitment to providing a practical guide for readers of varying skill levels involves a multi-faceted approach. It encompasses an understanding of the diverse audience, a layered learning structure, hands-on application, real-world relevance, adaptability, interactive elements, expert insights, and continuous support. This commitment ensures that the book becomes not just a source of information but a catalyst for practical proficiency in TOR, Kali Linux, ethical hacking, and digital fortification. By adhering to these principles, the book aims to empower readers with the skills and knowledge necessary to navigate the complexities of cybersecurity effectively.

CHAPTER 1: UNDERSTANDING TOR: THE FOUNDATION OF ANONYMITY

As we embark on the journey into the intricate world of cybersecurity, Chapter 1 serves as the gateway to a fundamental pillar of online anonymity—The Onion Router, more commonly known as TOR. This chapter is dedicated to unraveling the mysteries surrounding TOR, exploring its basics, architecture, and the principles that underpin the achievement of online anonymity. In this foundational chapter, readers will be guided through the essential concepts, providing a robust understanding of TOR's role as the bedrock of digital privacy.

TOR Ecosystem: Where Privacy Peels Back Like an Onion

Imagine a world where browsing the internet doesn't feel like walking through a crowded marketplace, your every click and glance scrutinized by unseen eyes. Enter Tor, a digital labyrinth where your online footprints dissolve with each twist and turn. Its very name, an acronym for The Onion Router, hints at its intricate architecture, where layers of encryption peel back like the skin of an onion, unveiling anonymity at its core.

In simpler terms, Tor is a free and open-source software that protects your internet traffic from prying eyes. It does this by routing your data through a network of volunteer-run relays, each one cloaking your destination and obscuring your true origin. Think of it as a multi-layered cloak woven from cryptography, where your data hopscotch across the globe, shedding identifiers with each leap, until it finally reaches its intended recipient, leaving nothing but digital breadcrumbs pointing nowhere.

But why would anyone need such a cloak? Let's examine the landscape of the digital world:

- Surveillance Capitalism: Corporations and governments alike track our online activities, building intricate profiles used for targeted advertising, influencing our behavior, and potentially even infringing on our privacy.

- Censorship and Oppression: In countries with restrictive regimes, accessing certain information or voicing dissent online can be dangerous. Tor empowers individuals to circumvent these limitations and exercise their right to free speech.

- Digital Threats: Journalists, activists, and whistleblowers face heightened risks online. Tor can shield them from targeted attacks and ensure their safety while they expose injustices.

This doesn't mean Tor is solely for the fringes of the internet. Anyone concerned about their online privacy can benefit from its protection. Whether you're a casual user wary of targeted ads, a journalist seeking secure communication, or simply someone who values unfettered access to information, Tor offers a powerful tool for reclaiming your digital sovereignty.

So, how does this onion-peeling magic work? The core of Tor lies in its architecture:

- Entry Nodes: Your journey begins at an entry node, one of thousands of volunteer-run servers scattered across the globe. It receives your encrypted data and passes it on to the next layer.

- Middle Nodes (Relays): Your data then bounces through several "middle nodes," each one further obfuscating its origin by stripping away another layer of encryption. These relays act as blind intermediaries, unaware of your final destination or your true identity.

- Exit Nodes: Finally, your data emerges from the last "exit node," connecting to the website you requested. This node acts as the final peel, allowing you to interact with the internet while cloaked in Tor's protective layers.

Remember, each node only sees the information passed directly to it, never the full picture. This multi-hop relay system, coupled with strong encryption, leaves would-be trackers clutching at digital shadows.

But Tor is not just about hiding in the shadows. It's also about building a more open and accessible internet. Its infrastructure relies on thousands of volunteers offering their bandwidth and resources to support this digital haven. This creates a vibrant ecosystem where developers contribute code, researchers analyze the network's strengths and weaknesses, and advocacy groups fight for its continued existence.

In this chapter, we will peel back the layers of Tor, exploring its technical mechanisms, delving into its diverse applications, and examining the challenges and controversies surrounding its use. Join us on this journey through the hidden corners of the internet, where anonymity reigns and privacy blooms like a delicate onion flower.

Decoding TOR: **More Than an Acronym**

Beyond the simple acronym, "The Onion Router," lies a tapestry of hidden meanings, reflecting the multifaceted nature of Tor. Just as an onion reveals its complexity layer by layer, so too does Tor unveil its capabilities through a deeper understanding of its name.

Unveiling the Layers:

- The: Defiance and Ownership: The definite article, "The," imbues Tor with a sense of definitive existence, a defiant stance against the pervasiveness of online surveillance. It declares Tor not as a fleeting option, but as a established force for privacy within the digital landscape.

- Onion: Layered Protection: The core metaphor, "onion," is where Tor's essence truly shines. Each layer of an onion represents a level of encryption, a protective barrier safeguarding your data as it traverses the Tor network. Just as peeling back an onion reveals hidden depths, understanding the "onion router" analogy unlocks the intricate mechanism of Tor's encryption.

- Router: Pathfinding in the Dark: The final word, "router," signifies Tor's function as a digital pathfinder. It navigates the internet's labyrinthine pathways, not on the well-lit highways, but through hidden alleyways and concealed tunnels. This "routing" metaphor emphasizes Tor's ability to cloak your online footprints, leaving only faint echoes in the digital ether.

Beyond the Acronym:

The name "Tor" is not merely a convenient label; it embodies the network's core principles and functionalities. It whispers promises of anonymous exploration, veiled communication, and a resistance to the panoptic gaze of online trackers.

Tools for a Diverse Landscape:

Tor's multifaceted nature caters to a diverse audience with varied needs:

- Privacy Purists: For those seeking absolute anonymity, Tor offers a haven, shielding their online activities from prying eyes. Journalists facing digital threats, activists battling censorship, and whistleblowers exposing injustices find in Tor a shield against retaliation.

- Security-Conscious Citizens: Even non-tech-savvy individuals concerned about targeted advertising and data collection can harness Tor's power. It empowers them to reclaim control over their online footprints, browse the internet without feeling like a lab rat in a marketing experiment, and safeguard their personal information from unwanted intrusions.

- Digital Freedom Fighters: Tor serves as a beacon of hope for those advocating for a free and open internet. It bypasses geographical restrictions and censorship filters, providing access to information and platforms otherwise shrouded in darkness.

Navigating the Gray Areas

While Tor champions privacy, its inherent anonymity attracts controversy. Some argue that it facilitates illegal activities, harboring criminal activities in its hidden corners. However, it's crucial to remember that technology, like any tool, can be misused. Tor itself is neutral, just as a hammer can be used to build a house or break a window. The responsibility lies with the user.

Decoding the Message:

Understanding the layers of meaning embedded in "The Onion Router" is more than just deciphering an acronym. It's about appreciating the network's philosophy, its diverse applications, and its potential impact on the future of the internet. As we delve deeper into Tor's technical mechanisms, user stories, and ethical considerations in the following sections, remember that "The Onion Router" is not just a name; it's a whispered promise of digital freedom, anonymity, and a path less traveled in the bustling internet marketplace.

The TOR Ecosystem: Understanding Nodes and Circuits

In the intricate web of TOR, understanding its core components—nodes and circuits—is essential to unraveling the network's architecture and achieving online anonymity. Let's embark on a detailed exploration, breaking down the roles of relay nodes and the establishment of circuits to facilitate secure and anonymous communication. Through step-by-step explanations and visual aids, we aim to make these complex concepts accessible to readers of varying technical backgrounds.

The Foundation: Nodes as Relays

At the heart of TOR's functionality lies a network of nodes, acting as relays to facilitate the secure transfer of data. To grasp TOR's essence, we must first understand how these nodes operate.

1. Relay Nodes: The Backbone of TOR

Relay nodes form the backbone of the TOR network. Acting as intermediaries in the transmission of data, these nodes play a pivotal role in obscuring the origin of information. When a user initiates a request, the data is routed through a series of relay nodes before reaching its final destination. **Each relay node strips away a layer of encryption, progressively concealing the data's source.**

2. Entry Nodes: Initiating the TOR Journey

The journey of data within TOR commences with an entry node. This initial relay node is where a user's data enters the TOR network. The entry node encrypts the data and passes it on to the next relay node, marking the beginning of a secure and obfuscated journey through the TOR ecosystem.

3. Exit Nodes: Returning to the Clearnet

The final relay node in the TOR network is the exit node. Here, the encrypted data emerges from the TOR network and enters the clearnet—the regular, unencrypted internet. At this stage, the last layer of encryption is removed, and the data reaches its intended destination.

Establishing Secure Communication: **The Role of Circuits**

Nodes, while crucial, do not operate in isolation. They are dynamically connected through circuits, creating a secure and anonymous pathway for data transmission.

Understanding the establishment and function of circuits is crucial in comprehending how TOR provides a layered approach to online privacy.

1. Circuits: Dynamic Pathways Through TOR

Circuits within TOR are dynamic pathways that data follows through the relay nodes. When a user initiates a request, TOR dynamically selects a series of relay nodes to form a circuit for that specific data transfer. **This selection is not only automatic but also changes periodically,** enhancing the resilience of TOR's security.

2. Encryption Layers: Building a Protective Shield

As data traverses through the circuit of relay nodes, **it is enveloped in multiple layers of encryption.** Each relay node in the circuit peels away one layer, decrypting only the information necessary to route the data to its next destination. By the time the data reaches the exit node, the last layer of encryption is removed, and the information is delivered to its intended endpoint.

3. Ensuring Anonymity: Randomized Circuit Selection

TOR enhances anonymity by employing a randomized approach to circuit selection. Each time a user makes a request, TOR dynamically selects a different set of relay nodes for the circuit, ensuring that the pathway for data transmission is unpredictable. **This randomization is a fundamental aspect of TOR's commitment to anonymity.**

Visual Aids and Illustrative Diagrams: **Enhancing Comprehension**

Recognizing the complexity of these concepts, let's enrich our understanding with visual aids and illustrative diagrams.

1. Relay Node Dance: A Visual Representation

2. Dynamic TOR Circuits: An Illustration

3. Encryption Layers: Visualizing Protection

Navigating TOR's Ecosystem with Confidence

In conclusion, our exploration of TOR's ecosystem of nodes and circuits is a foundational step in understanding the intricacies of this renowned privacy network. By unraveling the role of relay nodes as they dance with data and comprehending the dynamic pathways of circuits that secure communication, you are now equipped with a profound understanding of TOR's architecture. Visual aids and illustrative diagrams have played a pivotal role in making these concepts tangible, allowing you to navigate TOR's ecosystem with confidence as you delve deeper into the realms of online anonymity and digital security.

Navigating the Basics of TOR Usage

Now that you've unwrapped the core principles of TOR, let's peel back the first layer and delve into its practical application. We'll embark on a guided journey through setting up and using TOR, ensuring even those with minimal tech experience can navigate this digital labyrinth with confidence.

Step 1: Unmasking the "Entry Point": Downloading TOR Browser

Your first stop is the official website of the Tor Project: https://www.torproject.org/download/tor/. Here, amidst the sea of information, you'll find the key to unlocking anonymity – the Tor Browser. Choose the version compatible with your operating system (Windows, Mac, Linux, or even Android!) and download it. Remember, only trust the official website to avoid downloading malware disguised as legitimate software.

Step 2: Unveiling the Gateway: Installing and Launching

Once downloaded, follow the installation instructions, which are just as straightforward as installing any other browser. Once complete, launch the Tor Browser. Don't be surprised by its familiar Firefox-like interface; this deliberate design choice eases the learning curve for users accustomed to traditional browsers.

Step 3: Reaching for the Cloak: Connecting to the TOR Network

Now comes the magic – connecting to the Tor network. Click the onion icon in the address bar, and a window titled "Tor Connection" will appear. Click the Connect button, and watch the progress bar fill as Tor establishes its layered pathway through the network. Don't worry if it takes a few seconds; anonymity doesn't come without a bit of patience.

Step 4: Browsing in the Shadows: Exploring the Web with TOR

Once connected, the "Congratulations! You Are Now Using Tor" message heralds your entry into the realm of anonymity. Now, you can browse the internet just as you would with any other browser. Visit your favorite websites, check your email, or engage in social media – all under the protective cloak of Tor.

Bonus Tips for Enhanced Anonymity:

- HTTPS Everywhere: Enable the HTTPS Everywhere add-on for encrypted connections to websites, further fortifying your privacy.

- NoScript: Consider using NoScript to disable potentially invasive JavaScript on websites, preventing tracking scripts from compromising your anonymity.

- Security Settings: Explore Tor Browser's built-in security settings to adjust the level of protection based on your needs.

Remember: While Tor offers robust anonymity, it's not foolproof. Avoid downloading suspicious files, and maintain basic online hygiene practices, like using strong passwords and avoiding sharing sensitive information on unencrypted platforms.

Embrace the Journey:

Navigating the basics of TOR usage is a simple yet empowering experience. With each click within the Tor Browser, you're taking control of your online footprint, reclaiming your privacy in a world increasingly hungry for your data. This is just the first step on your journey through the onion layers; future sections will delve deeper into advanced techniques, explore specific use cases, and discuss the ethical considerations surrounding this powerful technology. So, open your Tor Browser, embrace the anonymity, and let's explore the hidden corners of the internet together.

TOR Installation: A Step-by-Step Guide

Welcome to your path less traveled on the internet, where anonymity awaits beyond the first layer of the onion! This section equips you with a step-by-step guide to installing the Tor Browser, your trusty cloak for navigating the digital shadows. Fear not, tech ninjas and beginners alike – we'll peel back the complexity and unveil a straightforward journey towards secure browsing.

Step 1: Charting Your Course – Downloading the Tor Browser

1. Set sail to the source: Open your trusty web browser (any will do for now!) and navigate to the official Tor Project
website: https://www.torproject.org/download/.

2. Choose your weapon: Look for the Download Tor Browser section. From the dropdown menu, select your operating system (Windows, Mac, Linux, or even Android!). Remember, downloading from the official website ensures you're not inviting digital gremlins onto your device.

Step 2: Building Your Stronghold – Installing the Tor Browser

1. Unveiling the treasure: Locate the downloaded file (usually in your Downloads folder) and double-click to open it. Follow the on-screen instructions, which will be tailored to your specific operating system. Most of the time, it's as simple as clicking "Next" a few times.

2. Choosing your haven: Depending on your system, you might be asked where you want to install the Tor Browser. We recommend sticking to the default location unless you have a specific reason to change it.

Step 3: Raising the Drawbridge – Launching the Tor Browser

1. Seek the onion icon: Once the installation is complete, you'll find a new resident on your device – the Tor Browser! Look for its distinct orange onion icon in your Start Menu (Windows), Applications folder (Mac), or wherever you find your installed programs.

2. Step into the shadows: Double-click the Tor Browser icon. You'll be greeted by a welcoming message and the "Tor Connection" window. Don't be surprised if it takes a few moments to establish your connection; remember, anonymity takes a bit of patience.

Congratulations! You've successfully installed the Tor Browser and taken your first step towards exploring the internet with enhanced privacy.

Bonus Tip: To verify your connection to the Tor network, click the onion icon in the Tor Browser address bar and select "Check my Tor exit nodes." This will reveal the current path your data is taking, confirming your anonymity is in place.

Remember, this is just the beginning of your journey through the onion layers. Stay tuned for the next sections, where we'll delve deeper into using the Tor Browser effectively, explore its diverse applications, and navigate the ethical considerations surrounding this powerful tool for online privacy. So, open your Tor Browser, embrace the invisibility, and let's continue peeling back the secrets of the internet together!

TOR Configuration: **Tailoring Anonymity to Your Needs**

Configuring TOR to align with your privacy preferences is a pivotal step in maximizing its effectiveness as a tool for secure and anonymous browsing. In this section, we will guide you through the TOR configuration settings, offering practical tips and recommendations to empower you to customize your TOR experience based on your specific anonymity requirements. By the end of this exploration, you'll not only understand the nuances of TOR configuration but also be equipped to adapt TOR to suit your individual preferences effortlessly.

Understanding TOR Configuration

Before diving into the configuration settings, let's establish a foundational understanding of what TOR configuration entails. Think of TOR configuration as fine-tuning a musical instrument to produce the desired melody. In the digital realm, it involves adjusting TOR's settings to harmonize with your privacy needs. Whether you're a privacy-conscious individual, a journalist protecting sources, or someone exploring the depths of the internet, TOR configuration allows you to tailor your experience.

Navigating to TOR's Settings

1. **Open the TOR Browser:** Begin by launching the TOR browser on your device. If you haven't installed TOR yet, make sure to follow the installation steps provided in Chapter 1.

2. **Access the Settings:** In the TOR browser, click on the three horizontal lines in the top-right corner to open the menu. From the dropdown menu, select

"Preferences" or "Options" based on your operating system.

3. **Explore the TOR Settings:** Within the settings menu, you'll find various categories, each corresponding to different aspects of TOR's functionality. Our focus will be on the privacy and security settings, but feel free to explore other sections to familiarize yourself with TOR's customization options.

Privacy Settings: **Anonymity at Your Fingertips**

1. **Security Level: Balancing Privacy and Functionality**

- **Adjusting the Security Slider:** TOR offers a security slider that allows you to balance privacy and functionality. The slider ranges from low to high, with each level offering different trade-offs. A low-security setting provides a more lenient browsing experience, while a high-security setting enhances privacy at the cost of some web functionality.

- **Recommended Setting:** For everyday browsing, a medium or high security level is recommended to ensure robust privacy. Experiment with the slider and find the level that best suits your needs.

2. Privacy and Security Preferences: Customizing Your TOR Experience

- **Cookies and Tracking:** Customize how TOR handles cookies and tracking scripts. You can choose to block third-party cookies, preventing advertisers from tracking your online behavior.

- **Javascript:** Consider disabling Javascript for additional privacy. While this may affect the functionality of some websites, it enhances your protection against certain online threats.

- **Search Engine Choices:** TOR provides privacy-focused search engine options. Explore the available choices and select one that aligns with your preferences for anonymous searches.

Security Settings: **Strengthening Your Digital Fortress**

1. Network Security: Safeguarding Your Connection

- **Bridge Configuration:** If you're in a region where TOR access is restricted or monitored, configure bridges to bypass censorship. Bridges disguise your TOR traffic, making it harder for adversaries to detect.

- **HTTPS Everywhere:** Enable the "HTTPS Everywhere" option to ensure that your connections to websites are encrypted whenever possible.

- **Security Certificates:** Regularly check for and update security certificates. This ensures that your TOR browser recognizes secure connections, protecting you from potential security vulnerabilities.

Advanced Settings: **Tailoring TOR to Your Preferences**

1. Advanced Security Settings: A Deeper Dive

- **NoScript Configuration:** NoScript is a powerful tool that allows you to control which scripts are allowed to run on websites. While it might impact website functionality, it significantly enhances security.

- **Circuit Display:** Enable the circuit display feature to visualize the path your data takes through the TOR network. This adds a layer of transparency to your TOR usage.

- **Customizing Security Preferences:** Explore advanced security preferences to fine-tune your TOR experience. This may include adjusting security protocols and encryption algorithms based on your technical comfort and requirements.

Recommendations for Tailoring TOR

1. **Regularly Review and Update Settings:** The digital landscape is dynamic, and so are the threats it poses. Regularly revisit your TOR settings to ensure they align with the current state of online privacy and security.

2. **Experiment with Different Configurations:** TOR provides a range of customization options. Don't hesitate to experiment with different configurations to find the balance between privacy and functionality that suits your browsing habits.

3. **Stay Informed About Updates:** TOR developers regularly release updates to enhance security and privacy features. Stay informed about these updates and promptly integrate them into your TOR browser for optimal protection.

4. **Join TOR Communities:** Engage with the TOR community to learn from others' experiences and gather insights into effective configuration strategies. The TOR community is a valuable resource for staying abreast of best practices and emerging threats.

Conclusion: Empowering Your TOR Experience

In conclusion, configuring TOR is not a one-size-fits-all endeavor; it's a personalized journey that empowers you to tailor your online anonymity. By navigating TOR's settings, adjusting privacy preferences, and experimenting with different configurations, you take control of your digital privacy destiny. TOR configuration isn't just a technical task; it's an ongoing process that evolves with your needs and the ever-changing digital landscape. As you delve into the myriad settings, remember that each adjustment brings you one step closer to a personalized and fortified TOR experience, aligning with your unique requirements and preferences.

Principles of Achieving Online Anonymity: Peeling Back the Layers of Privacy

Now that you've donned your Tor cloak and embarked on your anonymous journey, let's delve deeper into the principles that guide your path. We'll explore the layered approach to security, acknowledge potential pitfalls, and celebrate the ongoing evolution of Tor in the face of ever-changing digital threats.

The Layered Approach: Understanding TOR's Security Layers

Imagine peeling back an onion: with each layer, you reveal a hidden depth. Tor's anonymity works similarly, relying on multiple layers of protection to safeguard your digital identity.

1. Encryption: At the core lies encryption. Tor encrypts your data multiple times, creating a series of digital envelopes that cloak your information as it travels through the network. Think of it as nesting Russian dolls of privacy – each layer adding another barrier to prying eyes.

2. The "Onion Router" Analogy: Then comes the magic of the relays. Just like the layers of an onion, your data hopscotch across a network of volunteer-run relays, each one obscuring its origin by stripping away another layer of encryption. Imagine blindfolded messengers passing your data anonymously, none of them knowing its ultimate destination or your true identity.

3. Exit Nodes: Finally, your data emerges through an exit node, its final peel before reaching its destination. This node acts as the last anonymous intermediary, connecting you to your desired website while keeping your location and browsing habits hidden.

By understanding these layered protections, you gain confidence in Tor's robustness as a privacy tool. Remember, anonymity isn't about being invisible; it's about making it virtually impossible for anyone to track your activities or pinpoint your location.

Pitfalls and Precautions: **Navigating the Challenges of Anonymity**

While Tor empowers your online freedom, it's crucial to acknowledge potential pitfalls:

1. JavaScript Tracking: Some websites utilize JavaScript to track user behavior. To maximize anonymity, consider using browser extensions like NoScript to disable scripts on untrusted websites.

2. Exit Node Risks: Exit nodes act as the final point of contact with the open internet. While the majority are reliable, some might be compromised. To mitigate this risk, consider using Tor bridges, specialized relays that further anonymize your traffic before entering the Tor network.

3. Download with Caution: Malicious files can compromise your anonymity even within Tor. Stick to trusted sources and exercise caution when downloading files.

Remember, awareness is key. By acknowledging the limitations of Tor and adopting preventive measures, you navigate the digital landscape with a clear understanding of the risks and your role in maintaining your privacy.

TOR's Evolution: Adapting to Emerging Challenges

The digital landscape is a constantly evolving battlefield, with new threats and challenges emerging around every corner. To remain an effective shield for online privacy, Tor undergoes continuous refinement and development.

1. Research and Development: The Tor Project actively researches and implements new technologies to strengthen anonymity and address emerging vulnerabilities. This ongoing commitment ensures Tor adapts to meet the ever-changing digital threats.

2. Community Collaboration: The Tor community plays a crucial role in development and testing. Open-source contributors volunteer their skills and expertise to identify and address potential weaknesses, making Tor a truly collaborative effort for global digital privacy.

By understanding TOR's ongoing evolution, you gain confidence in its resilience and appreciate the dedication of the developers and community who safeguard your online freedom.

Remember, achieving online anonymity requires a layered approach, awareness of potential pitfalls, and an appreciation for Tor's continuous adaptation. By embracing these principles, you navigate the digital world with confidence, reclaiming your privacy and shaping a future where anonymity empowers true online freedom.

Stay tuned for the upcoming sections, where we'll explore specific use cases for Tor, delve into the ethical considerations surrounding its use, and discover the exciting future of privacy technologies.

Chapter 1 serves as a comprehensive initiation into the realm of TOR, laying the groundwork for readers to comprehend its basics, architecture, and the principles that facilitate online anonymity. By decoding the TOR ecosystem, guiding users through practical usage, and exploring the underlying principles, this chapter establishes a solid foundation for the journey ahead. As readers delve into subsequent chapters, armed with a profound understanding of TOR, you will be poised to navigate the complexities of cybersecurity with enhanced confidence and privacy.

CHAPTER 2: DEEP WEB NAVIGATION: A PRACTICAL GUIDE

The internet you know - with its search engines and familiar websites - is just the tip of the iceberg. Beneath it lies the deep web, a vast and vibrant ecosystem of hidden content accessible only through specialized tools like Tor. This chapter serves as your compass, guiding you through the uncharted waters of deep web exploration, highlighting its potential benefits and risks, and equipping you with the knowledge to navigate safely and responsibly.

Unveiling the Deep Web: Beyond the Search Engines

Think of the internet as a massive library. The surface level showcases popular books and magazines, easily discoverable through library catalogs. The deep web, however, holds the rare manuscripts, archived documents, and hidden publications – accessible only through specific knowledge and specialized keys. These hidden pages, accessible only through special software like Tor and specific links called onion addresses, constitute the deep web.

Diving Deep: Benefits of Exploring the Deep Web

Venturing into the deep web is not about seeking nefarious activities. It boasts diverse and legitimate benefits:

- Academic Research: Unrestricted access to academic journals, scholarly articles, and historical documents not found on conventional search engines.

- Freedom of Expression: Platforms for marginalized voices and whistleblowers to share information without fear of censorship or persecution.

- Privacy Protection: Secure communication platforms and tools that shield your online activities from surveillance and data collection.

- Alternative Marketplaces: Access to niche markets for specialized goods and services not found on mainstream platforms.

Navigating the Depths: Practical Tips for Safety

The deep web, like any unexplored territory, requires caution and vigilance. Here are some practical tips for safe navigation:

- Trustworthy Entry Points: Stick to reputable Tor onion addresses recommended by trusted sources. Avoid clicking on unknown links, as they might lead to malicious or fraudulent websites.

- Strong Cybersecurity: Maintain robust antivirus and anti-malware software. Avoid downloading files from untrusted sources, as they might contain hidden malware.

- Digital Hygiene: Use strong passwords and practice basic online security measures, like two-factor authentication, across all deep web platforms.

- Anonymity Mindset: Remember, even inside the deep web, complete anonymity is difficult to achieve. Be cautious about sharing sensitive information and maintain awareness of potential risks.

Potential Risks: Recognizing the Dark Side of the Deep Web

It's important to acknowledge that the deep web is not a utopian haven. Be aware of these potential risks:

- Illegal Activities: Some areas of the deep web harbor illegal activities like drug trafficking, weapons sales, and black markets. Avoid these areas and report any suspicious activity.

- Scams and Fraud: Deceptive practices like phishing scams and fake marketplaces are prevalent. Remain vigilant and exercise caution when interacting with unknown entities.

- Malware and Hacking: Malicious actors may exploit vulnerabilities in deep web software. Stay updated on security patches and avoid suspicious downloads.

Ethical Considerations: Responsible Exploration in the Deep Web

With great freedom comes great responsibility. Before embarking on your deep web journey, consider these ethical guidelines:

- Respect Privacy: Do not engage in activities that might compromise the privacy of others, such as hacking or unauthorized data collection.

- Support Legitimate Uses: Advocate for and support platforms and initiatives that promote positive and ethical uses of the deep web.

- Report Misconduct: If you encounter illegal or unethical activities, report them to the appropriate authorities and help clean up the digital landscape.

Remember, the deep web is a powerful tool, and like any tool, its value depends on its user. By approaching it with caution, awareness, and a commitment to ethical exploration, you can reap the benefits of this hidden internet realm while contributing to a safer and more responsible digital future.

This chapter serves as a foundation for further exploration in subsequent sections. You can delve deeper into specific aspects of deep web navigation, such as using onion addresses, finding reputable platforms, or understanding the technical complexities of accessing hidden content. Always remember to approach the deep web with a healthy dose of curiosity, caution, and ethical responsibility.

I hope this comprehensive version of Chapter 2 equips you with the knowledge and tools to navigate the deep web safely and responsibly. Remember, stay tuned for the upcoming sections, where we'll explore specific applications, legal and ethical considerations, and exciting possibilities for the future of this hidden corner of the internet.

Chapter 3: Kali Linux Essentials

Tools for Security Warriors

Forget the shiny armor and castle walls of medieval knights. In the realm of cybersecurity, your weapons are your wits, your knowledge, and a powerful arsenal of tools at your fingertips. Enter Kali Linux, your digital broadsword and enchanted shield, your code-forged crossbow and knowledge-crafted helmet. This chapter equips you with the essentials of this ethical hacking toolkit, transforming you from a curious observer into a security warrior ready to protect the digital domain.

Unveiling the Warrior's Code

What is Kali Linux?

Kali Linux isn't your average operating system. It's a Debian-based platform specifically designed for penetration testing and security auditing. Think of it as your digital war room, pre-loaded with a vast array of tools for:

- Vulnerability Scanning: Identify weaknesses in network systems and software before malicious actors exploit them.

- Password Cracking: Test the strength of passwords and uncover potential security vulnerabilities.

- Wireless Network Security: Analyze and test the security of Wi-Fi networks, ensuring your own connection remains impregnable.

- Web Application Security: Identify and exploit vulnerabilities in websites and web applications to patch them before attackers strike.

- Social Engineering: Understand the tactics used by cybercriminals to deceive and manipulate, better equipping yourself to resist their tricks.

Hands-on Training

Mastering Essential Kali Tools

This isn't a spectator sport. Let's dive into the heart of the tools that will hone your security skills:

- Nmap: Your digital cartographer, mapping out networks and discovering their vulnerabilities.

- Wireshark: Your network eavesdropper, capturing and analyzing data packets to uncover hidden threats.

- Metasploit: Your digital arsenal, housing a vast collection of exploits and tools to simulate real-world attacks.

- John the Ripper: Your password cracker, testing the strength of passwords and exposing potential weaknesses.

- Social-Engineer Toolkit (SET): Your deception detector, teaching you to recognize and disarm the tricks of social engineering attacks.

Practice Makes Perfect

Setting Up Your Kali Training Ground

Before venturing into the digital battlefield, you need a training ground. Here's how to set up your own secure learning environment:

- Install Kali Linux: Choose your platform (virtual machine, dedicated machine, dual boot) and follow the installation guide.

- Get Familiar with the Interface: Explore the Kali desktop, learn basic commands, and understand the file system.

- Start with Beginner-Friendly Tools: Nmap and Wireshark are excellent entry points to network scanning and analysis.

- Practice in a Controlled Environment: Use dedicated training platforms like VulnHub and HackTheBox to hone your skills without harming real-world systems.

The Path of the Ethical Hacker

Responsible Use of Kali Linux

Remember, with great power comes great responsibility. Kali Linux is a powerful tool, and its misuse can have dire consequences. Use it ethically and responsibly:

- Always obtain permission: Never try to hack or exploit systems without explicit consent from the owner.

- Respect the law: Hacking into unauthorized systems is illegal and can lead to serious legal repercussions.

- Use your skills for good: Protect yourself, your loved ones, and your organization from cyber threats.

- Contribute to the community: Share your knowledge and skills to help others improve their cybersecurity posture.

Beyond the Basics:

Deepening Your Security Expertise

This chapter is just the first step on your journey as a security warrior. The Kali Linux arsenal holds countless tools and techniques waiting to be explored. Remember:

- Join the Community: Connect with other security professionals, learn from their experiences, and contribute to the collective knowledge base.

- Specialize Your Skills: Develop a specific area of expertise, whether it's network security, web application security, or social engineering defense.

The digital world needs guardians, defenders of cyberspace, warriors wielding the power of knowledge and technology. With Kali Linux by your side, you have the tools to become one of them. Sharpen your code-forged blades, hone your analytical skills, and stand ready to protect the digital realm from those who seek to exploit it.

You've chosen the path of Kali Linux, the powerful hacking toolkit that will sharpen your skills and equip you to defend the digital frontier. This guide is your launchpad, propelling you from curious observer to proficient security warrior. Let's dive in!

1. Downloading Kali Linux:

Official   Website:
https://www.kali.org/docs/introduction/download-official-kali-linux-images/

Here, you'll find various download options depending on your platform:

- Virtual Machine: Run Kali in a virtual environment alongside your existing operating system. Ideal for beginners and experimentation. Download the ISO file and use software like VirtualBox or VMware to create your virtual machine.

- Live Boot: Try Kali without installing it, useful for testing tools or fixing a compromised system. Download the ISO file and burn it to a USB drive using Etcher or Rufus.

- Bare Metal Installation: Install Kali directly on your system, recommended for experienced users.

Bonus Tip: For the latest updates and greatest stability, choose the "kali-linux-rolling-SHA256SUMS.asc" and "kali-linux-*.iso" files.

2. Setting Up Your Training Ground:

Once downloaded, follow the installation guide specific to your chosen method. Here are some helpful resources:

- Virtual Machine: https://www.kali.org/docs/virtualization/install-virtualbox-guest-vm/

- Live Boot: https://www.kali.org/docs/usb/live-usb-install-with-windows/

- Bare Metal Installation: https://www.kali.org/docs/installation/hard-disk-install/

3. Mastering Essential Tools:

Kali Linux comes pre-loaded with a vast arsenal of tools. Start with some beginner-friendly options:

- Nmap: Network scanner – https://nmap.org/

- Wireshark: Network traffic analyzer – https://www.wireshark.org/

- John the Ripper: Password cracker – https://www.openwall.com/lists/john-users/

- Social-Engineer Toolkit (SET): Social engineering framework – https://github.com/trustedsec/social-engineer-toolkit

Practice makes perfect! Use dedicated training platforms like VulnHub (https://www.vulnhub.com/) and HackTheBox (https://www.hackthebox.com/) to hone your skills without harming real-world systems.

4. Ethical Hacking Principles:

Remember, great power comes with great responsibility. Always use Kali Linux ethically:

- Never hack without permission.

- Respect the law.

- Use your skills for good.

- Contribute to the community.

5. Deepening Your Expertise:

This is just the beginning! Stay updated with the latest threats, vulnerabilities, and tools through resources like:

- Kali   Linux
  Documentation: https://www.kali.org/docs/

- Offensive Security: https://www.offsec.com/courses-and-certifications/

- Kali Tools: https://www.kali.org/tools/all-tools/

Join the community! Share your knowledge, learn from others, and contribute to the collective defense of the digital world.

Remember, the journey to becoming a skilled security warrior is a continuous one. Embrace the challenge, stay curious, and keep learning!

Ready to unleash the Kali warrior within? Download Kali Linux now, follow these steps, and embark on your exciting journey towards mastering the tools and techniques of ethical hacking. The digital frontier awaits!

CHAPTER 4: ETHICAL HACKING: A RESPONSIBLE APPROACH

In the bustling digital landscape, security isn't merely a passive shield; it's a constant game of cat and mouse, a never-ending dance between attackers and defenders. Enter the ethical hacker, not a shadowy figure lurking in the digital shadows, but a white knight wielding the tools of vulnerability to strengthen the walls that protect our precious data. This chapter delves into the world of ethical hacking, equipping you with the knowledge and tools to be a responsible defender in the digital realm.

The Defender's Code:

What is Ethical Hacking?

Ethical hacking, unlike its malicious counterpart, isn't about exploiting vulnerabilities for personal gain. It's a proactive approach, a simulated siege on your own systems, conducted with explicit permission, to identify and patch weaknesses before malicious actors can exploit them. Think of it as stress-testing your digital fortress, exposing cracks in the foundation so you can repair them before a real attack.

The Tools of the White Hat

Methodology and Frameworks

Just like any knight needs their trusty armour and steed, the ethical hacker has their arsenal of tools and methodologies. Here's a glimpse into their toolkit:

- Reconnaissance: Gathering information about the target system, such as operating systems, network topology, and installed software. Tools like Nmap and OSINT frameworks help paint a detailed picture of the digital landscape.

- Vulnerability Scanning: Identifying weaknesses in the system using automated tools like Nessus or OpenVAS. Think of it as combing through the castle walls, searching for loose bricks or hidden cracks.

- Exploitation and Penetration Testing: Using simulated attacks, ethical hackers exploit identified vulnerabilities to understand their potential impact and gain access to the system. This is like testing the strength of the drawbridge with a battering ram, but in a controlled environment.

- Post-Exploitation and Reporting: Once inside the system, ethical hackers assess the potential damage an attacker could inflict and document their findings in a comprehensive report. It's like a detailed map of the conquered tower, highlighting its vulnerabilities and suggesting repairs.

The White Hat Way: Best Practices for Ethical Hacking

With great power comes great responsibility. Here are some essential best practices for ethical hackers:

- Always obtain explicit consent: Never hack a system without the owner's permission. Treat this as the most sacred rule of the white hat code.

- Respect the law: Adhere to all cybersecurity laws and regulations in your jurisdiction. Remember, even good intentions can have legal consequences if not conducted ethically.

- Document everything: Maintain detailed logs of your activities and findings to ensure transparency and accountability. Think of it as a detailed chronicle of your siege, ensuring everyone understands the process and outcome.

- Contribute to the community: Share your knowledge and findings with other ethical hackers to strengthen the collective defense against cyber threats. Remember, knowledge is power, and sharing strengthens the walls of the entire digital kingdom.

Beyond the Basics

Specializations and Opportunities

The world of ethical hacking is vast and diverse, offering a variety of specialization options:

- Web Application Security: Focus on identifying and exploiting vulnerabilities in websites and web applications.

- Network Security: Master the art of securing networks and identifying potential entry points for attackers.

- Social Engineering: Understand the human element of security and learn how to defend against manipulation and deception tactics.

- Red Team/Blue Team Exercises: Participate in simulated cyberwarfare exercises, where red teams act as attackers and blue teams defend the systems.

Resources and Training

Equipping Yourself for the Digital Battlefield

To hone your skills and become a proficient ethical hacker, there are numerous resources available:

- Online Courses and Certifications: Organizations like Offensive Security ([https://www.offsec.com/]) and

EC-Council ([https://www.eccouncil.org/]) offer comprehensive training and certifications.

- Vulnerability Training Platforms: Try your hand at ethical hacking in a safe environment using platforms like VulnHub ([https://www.vulnhub.com/]) and HackTheBox ([https://www.hackthebox.com/]).

- Online Communities and Forums: Connect with other ethical hackers through platforms like Reddit's r/hacking and Stack Exchange's Information Security forum.

Whether you're a seasoned IT professional or simply curious about the world of ethical hacking, remember, knowledge is power. By understanding the tools and techniques of ethical hackers, you become a more informed defender, capable of safeguarding your own systems and contributing to a more secure digital future. So, embrace the white hat code, sharpen your skills, and join the ranks of those who stand guard against the shadows, ensuring the digital realm remains a safe and thriving space for all.

CHAPTER 5: PENETRATION TESTING: ASSESSING AND STRENGTHENING SECURITY

In the ever-evolving landscape of cybersecurity, the concept of penetration testing emerges as a crucial and proactive measure to assess and strengthen digital fortifications. In this chapter, we will delve into the fundamentals of penetration testing, providing you with a comprehensive understanding of its significance and practical applications. Through real-world examples and hands-on exercises, you will not only grasp the theoretical aspects but also gain the skills necessary to apply penetration testing techniques in real-world scenarios.

Understanding Penetration Testing

What is Penetration Testing?

Penetration testing, often referred to as ethical hacking, is a controlled and simulated cyberattack conducted with the explicit purpose of identifying vulnerabilities in a system, network, or application. This proactive measure allows organizations and individuals to discover and address potential weaknesses before malicious actors exploit them.

Why is Penetration Testing Important?

Hackers continually adapt their tactics, making it essential for organizations and individuals to stay one step ahead. Penetration testing provides a preemptive strike against potential breaches, helping fortify digital defenses and ensuring a resilient security posture.

Practical Examples

Unveiling the World of Penetration Testing

Scenario 1: Web Application Security Assessment

Consider a scenario where an organization has a web application that handles sensitive user data. A penetration test is initiated to assess the application's security.

1. **Reconnaissance:** The penetration tester starts by gathering information about the web application, identifying potential entry points, and understanding its architecture.

2. **Scanning:** Automated tools and manual techniques are employed to scan the application for vulnerabilities, such as SQL injection or cross-site scripting.

3. **Gaining Access:** Simulating an attacker, the penetration tester exploits vulnerabilities to gain

unauthorized access to the application, replicating potential real-world threats.

4. **Privilege Escalation:** Once inside, the tester attempts to escalate privileges, mimicking the tactics of a malicious actor seeking to gain unauthorized control over the system.

5. **Documentation and Remediation:** A detailed report is compiled, highlighting the vulnerabilities discovered, the methods employed, and recommendations for remediation. This documentation guides the organization in strengthening its web application security.

Scenario 2: Network Infrastructure Assessment

In another scenario, a company's network infrastructure is the focus of a penetration test.

1. **Mapping the Network:** The penetration tester maps the network, identifying devices, servers, and potential entry points.

2. **Vulnerability Assessment:** Automated tools and manual analysis are employed to identify vulnerabilities in network devices, such as routers, switches, and firewalls.

3. **Exploitation:** The penetration tester simulates an attack by exploiting vulnerabilities to gain access to the network. This may involve bypassing firewalls or compromising weakly protected devices.

4. **Lateral Movement:** Once inside the network, the tester explores lateral movement, simulating how an attacker might navigate through the organization's systems.

5. **Analysis and Reporting:** A comprehensive report is generated, outlining vulnerabilities, potential risks, and recommendations for improving the overall security of the network infrastructure.

Hands-On Exercises:

Building Your Penetration Testing Skills

To empower you with practical proficiency in penetration testing, let's embark on hands-on exercises designed to simulate real-world scenarios.

Exercise 1: Web Application Assessment

1. **Select a Web Application:** Choose a web application that you have permission to test. This could be a personal project or an open-source application.

2. **Conduct Reconnaissance:** Use tools like Nmap or manual methods to gather information about the application's architecture, endpoints, and potential vulnerabilities.

3. **Perform Scanning:** Utilize automated tools (such as OWASP ZAP or Burp Suite) to scan the web application for common vulnerabilities like SQL injection, cross-site scripting, or insecure file uploads.

4. **Simulate Exploitation:** Safely exploit the identified vulnerabilities, understanding the potential impact and the methods an attacker might employ.

5. **Document Findings:** Create a comprehensive report detailing the vulnerabilities discovered, the exploitation process, and recommendations for mitigating the identified risks.

Exercise 2: Network Infrastructure Assessment

1. **Set Up a Lab Environment:** Create a controlled network environment using virtual machines or dedicated hardware. Ensure you have permission to conduct penetration testing in this environment.

2. **Map the Network:** Utilize tools like Nmap or Wireshark to map the network, identifying devices, open ports, and potential vulnerabilities.

3. **Vulnerability Scanning:** Deploy tools like OpenVAS or Nessus to perform vulnerability scans on network devices, identifying weaknesses and potential entry points.

4. **Simulate Exploitation:** Safely exploit vulnerabilities on network devices, understanding the tactics an attacker might use to gain unauthorized access.

5. **Generate a Comprehensive Report:** Document your findings, including vulnerabilities, potential risks, and recommendations for enhancing the security of the network infrastructure.

Empowering You for Cybersecurity Challenges

As we conclude this exploration of penetration testing, you are now equipped with a foundational understanding of its importance and practical applications. The real-world examples and hands-on exercises provided are designed to empower you

CHAPTER 6: SECURING YOUR DIGITAL FORTRESS: BEST PRACTICES

In the labyrinth of the digital world, where threats lurk around every virtual corner, the imperative to fortify your digital fortress becomes paramount. This chapter serves as your comprehensive guide to best practices in securing your digital assets against a myriad of cyber threats. We will cover essential topics such as password management, encryption, and secure communication, empowering you to establish robust defenses and navigate the digital realm with confidence.

Understanding the Stakes: The Need for Digital Security

Why Digital Security Matters

In an era where digital interactions are ubiquitous, the protection of sensitive information has never been more critical. Cyber threats, ranging from phishing attacks to sophisticated malware, pose constant challenges to the security of our digital assets. Understanding the stakes is the first step towards building a proactive and resilient defense.

Password Management: The Gateway to Security

Creating Strong and Unique Passwords

1. **Avoid Common Password Pitfalls:** Steer clear of easily guessable passwords, such as "password123" or "123456." Opt for combinations of uppercase and lowercase letters, numbers, and symbols.

2. **Use Passphrases:** Consider using passphrases—sequences of words or a sentence. These are not only easier to remember but also more robust against brute-force attacks.

3. **Implement Two-Factor Authentication (2FA):** Enhance your account security by enabling 2FA wherever possible. This adds an additional layer of protection beyond the password.

4. **Password Managers:** Explore password manager tools to generate and store complex passwords securely. This eliminates the need to remember multiple passwords while ensuring strong credentials.

Encryption:

Safeguarding Your Digital Communications

Understanding the Basics of Encryption

1. **What is Encryption:** Encryption is the process of converting data into a secure code to prevent

unauthorized access. It ensures that only authorized parties can decipher and access the information.

2. **Implement HTTPS:** Ensure that websites you visit use HTTPS (Hypertext Transfer Protocol Secure) for encrypted communication.

3. **End-to-End Encryption:** Embrace messaging platforms and email services that offer end-to-end encryption. This ensures that only the intended recipient can decrypt and read your messages.

4. **Encrypting Files and Drives:** Secure sensitive files and entire drives with encryption tools. BitLocker for Windows and FileVault for macOS are examples of built-in encryption options.

Secure Communication:

Protecting Your Interactions

Establishing Safe Digital Conversations

1. **Choose Secure Messaging Apps:** Opt for messaging applications that prioritize security, such as Signal or Telegram. These platforms employ robust encryption protocols to safeguard your conversations.

2. **Email Security Practices:** Be cautious with email attachments and links. Avoid clicking on suspicious

links, and use email encryption when sharing sensitive information.

3. **Virtual Private Network (VPN):** Utilize VPNs to encrypt your internet connection and protect your online activities from prying eyes, especially when using public Wi-Fi networks.

4. **Secure Video Conferencing:** When engaging in video conferences, choose platforms with end-to-end encryption. Additionally, implement meeting passwords and control access to ensure secure virtual gatherings.

Regular Audits and Updates

Maintaining Vigilance

The Importance of Continuous Security Audits

1. **Regularly Review Security Settings:** Conduct periodic reviews of your security settings across devices, applications, and online accounts. Ensure that configurations align with the latest security standards.

2. **Update Software and Firmware:** Keep your operating system, software, and firmware up to date.

3. **Network Security Audits:** Periodically assess the security of your home network. Change default router passwords, enable WPA3 encryption, and review connected devices for any potential vulnerabilities.

4. **Educate Yourself Continuously:** Stay informed about the latest cybersecurity threats and best practices. Attend webinars, read reputable cybersecurity blogs, and participate in online forums to remain vigilant and well-informed.

Fortifying Your Digital Sanctuary

As we conclude this journey through best practices in securing your digital fortress, remember that cybersecurity is a dynamic and evolving landscape. Implementing these best practices is not a one-time task but an ongoing commitment to safeguarding your digital existence.

By mastering password management, understanding encryption principles, prioritizing secure communication, and maintaining continuous vigilance through regular audits, you establish a robust defense against a variety of cyber threats. Empower yourself with knowledge, embrace proactive security measures, and fortify your digital sanctuary against the ever-present challenges of the digital world.

Your digital fortress is only as strong as your commitment to its defense. Stay secure, stay vigilant!

CHAPTER 7: ADVANCED SECURITY STRATEGIES: STAYING AHEAD OF EMERGING THREATS

In the dynamic and ever-evolving realm of cybersecurity, staying one step ahead of emerging threats requires a proactive and forward-thinking approach. This chapter serves as a guide to advanced security strategies, exploring cutting-edge methodologies to fortify your defenses against the latest and most sophisticated cyber threats. We will delve into emerging trends and technologies that are shaping the cybersecurity landscape, empowering you to adapt to the rapidly changing digital security landscape.

The Need for Advanced Security Strategies

The Acceleration of Cyber Threats

As technology advances, so do the capabilities of malicious actors seeking to exploit vulnerabilities in digital ecosystems. Advanced security strategies are not just a choice but a necessity to counteract the accelerated pace of cyber threats. This chapter aims to equip you with the knowledge and tools to navigate this ever-evolving landscape.

Adaptive Defense Strategies

Understanding Adaptive Security

1. **Behavioral Analytics:** Implement advanced behavioral analytics to detect anomalies in user behavior and identify potential security incidents. Machine learning algorithms can analyze patterns and deviations, enhancing threat detection capabilities.

2. **User and Entity Behavior Analytics (UEBA):** UEBA focuses on monitoring user activities and entity interactions within an organization. By establishing baselines of normal behavior, it becomes easier to spot unusual or malicious activities that may indicate a security breach.

3. **Threat Intelligence Integration:** Integrate threat intelligence feeds into your security infrastructure. By staying informed about the latest threats and attack vectors, you can proactively adjust your defense strategies to counter emerging risks.

4. **Continuous Security Training:** Implement ongoing security awareness and training programs for employees. Educated and vigilant staff members are a critical line of defense against evolving social engineering and phishing attacks.

Zero Trust Architecture

Rethinking Perimeter Security

1. Beyond Perimeter Defense: Move away from traditional perimeter-based security models. Embrace a zero-trust architecture that treats every user and device as potentially untrusted, requiring verification regardless of their location within the network.

2. **Micro-Segmentation:** Implement micro-segmentation to create isolated segments within your network. This ensures that even if one segment is compromised, lateral movement is restricted, minimizing the impact of a potential breach.

3. **Continuous Authentication:** Shift from static, periodic authentication to continuous authentication methods. This may include biometric authentication, behavior analysis, or multi-factor authentication that adapts based on user activities.

4. **End-to-End Encryption:** Extend the use of end-to-end encryption not only to communications but also to data at rest. This ensures that even if a device is compromised, the encrypted data remains secure.

Artificial Intelligence and Machine Learning

Harnessing AI for Security

1. **Predictive Analysis:** Utilize machine learning algorithms for predictive analysis of potential security

threats. These algorithms can identify patterns indicative of an impending attack, enabling proactive defense measures.

2. **Automated Incident Response:** Implement AI-driven automated incident response systems. These systems can rapidly analyze and respond to security incidents in real-time, minimizing the impact of breaches.

3. **Threat Hunting with AI:** Leverage AI for threat hunting activities. Machine learning algorithms can sift through vast datasets to identify subtle indicators of compromise that may go unnoticed by traditional security measures.

4. **AI-Driven Security Orchestration:** Integrate AI-driven security orchestration platforms that automate complex security processes. This ensures a coordinated and efficient response to security incidents.

Quantum-Safe Encryption

Preparing for Quantum Threats

1. **Quantum Computing Risks:** Acknowledge the potential threat that quantum computing poses to current encryption algorithms. Quantum computers

could theoretically break widely used encryption methods, compromising the confidentiality of data.

2. **Post-Quantum Cryptography:** Explore and adopt post-quantum cryptographic algorithms that are resistant to quantum attacks. Prepare your organization for the future by gradually transitioning to quantum-safe encryption methods.

3. **Risk Assessment:** Conduct a risk assessment to identify the impact of quantum computing on your current cryptographic infrastructure. Develop a roadmap for migrating to quantum-safe encryption as part of your long-term security strategy.

4. **Collaborate and Stay Informed:** Engage with the cybersecurity community and industry experts to stay informed about developments in quantum computing and quantum-safe encryption. Collaboration can provide valuable insights into emerging standards and best practices.

Evolving in Tandem with Threats

As we conclude this exploration of advanced security strategies, it is essential to recognize that cybersecurity is an ongoing journey of adaptation. The landscape will continue to evolve, and threats will become increasingly sophisticated.

By embracing adaptive defense strategies, zero trust architectures, harnessing the power of artificial intelligence, and preparing for quantum threats, you position yourself to not only withstand current challenges but also evolve in tandem with emerging threats.

Stay curious, stay informed, and remain vigilant. Advanced security is not a destination; it's a continuous process of refinement and adaptation to an ever-changing digital landscape. As you integrate these advanced strategies into your cybersecurity arsenal, you fortify your defenses against the unknown and position yourself to thrive in the face of evolving cyber threats.

CHAPTER 8: ENSURING ETHICAL CONDUCT: NAVIGATING LEGAL AND MORAL BOUNDARIES

In the dynamic and ever-evolving field of cybersecurity, the importance of ethical conduct cannot be overstated. This chapter serves as a compass, guiding readers through the intricacies of ethical behavior in cybersecurity practices. We will emphasize the significance of maintaining high ethical standards and provide guidance on navigating legal and moral boundaries, especially in the realm of ethical hacking. By understanding the ethical considerations that underpin cybersecurity, you empower yourself to contribute positively to the digital world while staying within the bounds of legality and morality.

The Foundation of Ethical Conduct

Why Ethics Matter in Cybersecurity

1. **Building Trust:** Ethical behavior is the cornerstone of building trust within the cybersecurity community and the broader digital ecosystem. Trust is essential for collaboration and information sharing, which are critical aspects of effective cybersecurity.

2. **Protecting Privacy:** Ethical conduct ensures the protection of privacy rights and user data. Respecting privacy is not only a legal requirement but also a moral obligation to safeguard individuals from unwarranted intrusions.

3. **Maintaining Professionalism:** Upholding ethical standards contributes to the professionalism of the cybersecurity field. Ethical behavior fosters a positive reputation for individuals and organizations, enhancing credibility and reliability.

4. **Preserving Integrity:** Ethical conduct preserves the integrity of cybersecurity practitioners. It ensures that individuals act in alignment with moral principles, fostering a culture of responsibility and accountability.

The Landscape of Ethical Hacking

Understanding Ethical Hacking

1. **Permission and Consent:** Ethical hacking requires explicit permission and consent. Before engaging in any form of security testing, ensure that you have legal authorization from the relevant parties. Unauthorized testing is not only unethical but can lead to legal consequences.

2. **Scope Definition:** Clearly define the scope of your ethical hacking activities. Understand the limits of your authorization and refrain from probing beyond the agreed-upon boundaries. This ensures that your actions remain ethical and within legal constraints.

3. **Responsible Disclosure:** If you discover vulnerabilities during ethical hacking activities, practice responsible disclosure. Notify the relevant parties promptly and provide sufficient details to allow them to address the issues. This approach enhances overall cybersecurity without causing harm.

4. **Continuous Learning:** Stay informed about evolving ethical hacking practices and standards. Continuous learning ensures that your skills remain relevant, and you are aware of the latest ethical considerations in the cybersecurity landscape.

Navigating Legal Boundaries

Compliance with Laws and Regulations

1. **Data Protection Laws:** Familiarize yourself with data protection laws and regulations applicable to your region. Understand the legal obligations regarding the collection, storage, and processing of personal information.

2. **Authorization and Consent:** Ensure that your ethical hacking activities comply with legal requirements related to authorization and consent. Violating these principles can lead to legal repercussions and damage your professional standing.

3. **Intellectual Property Rights:** Respect intellectual property rights when conducting ethical hacking. Avoid unauthorized use or distribution of proprietary software, tools, or any other intellectual property that does not belong to you.

4. **Cybercrime Laws:** Stay informed about cybercrime laws that pertain to your activities. Unauthorized access to computer systems, data theft, or any malicious intent can lead to severe legal consequences.

Balancing Moral Considerations

Ethics Beyond the Law

1. **Human Impact Assessment:** Consider the potential impact of your actions on individuals and society. Ethical behavior goes beyond legal compliance and involves a moral consideration of the consequences of your actions on the human element.

2. **Social Responsibility:** Recognize your social responsibility as a cybersecurity practitioner. Contribute positively to the digital community by sharing knowledge, collaborating with peers, and participating in initiatives that promote cybersecurity awareness.

3. **Avoiding Harm:** Prioritize avoiding harm in your ethical hacking endeavors. Ensure that your actions do not result in damage to systems, data, or the reputation of individuals or organizations.

4. **Professional Integrity:** Uphold professional integrity by being transparent, honest, and accountable for your actions. Admit mistakes, learn from them, and strive to continuously improve your ethical conduct.

A Commitment to Ethical Excellence

In the realm of cybersecurity, ethical conduct is not just a guideline; it is a commitment to excellence. By prioritizing ethical behavior, you contribute to the overall integrity and trustworthiness of the cybersecurity community. Navigating legal and moral boundaries requires continuous awareness, responsibility, and a dedication to upholding the highest standards of ethical conduct.

As you embark on your journey in cybersecurity, remember that ethical excellence is not a constraint but a catalyst for positive change. It sets the foundation for a secure and trustworthy digital future. Stay ethical, stay vigilant, and contribute to a digital landscape built on principles of integrity and responsibility.

CONCLUSION

Crafting Your Digital Legacy

As we reach the culmination of the TOR Blueprint journey, it's essential to reflect on the knowledge gained and consider the profound impact it can have on crafting your digital legacy. This exploration into the intricacies of TOR, ethical hacking, advanced security strategies, and ethical conduct in cybersecurity has equipped you with the tools to navigate the digital landscape responsibly. Let's distill the key takeaways and inspire you to apply this newfound knowledge in creating a secure and ethical digital legacy.

Embracing TOR and Cybersecurity Wisdom

1. **Empowerment through TOR:** The TOR Blueprint has unraveled the mysteries of the TOR network, empowering you to navigate the deep web, understand Kali Linux, and engage in ethical hacking practices. The TOR ecosystem, with its emphasis on anonymity and security, provides a foundation for exploring the digital realm with confidence.

2. **Proactive Security Measures:** By delving into advanced security strategies, you've fortified your digital fortress against emerging threats. Adaptive defense strategies, zero trust architectures, artificial

intelligence, and quantum-safe encryption are now integral components of your cybersecurity arsenal.

3. **Ethical Conduct as a Guiding Principle:** The emphasis on ethical conduct in cybersecurity practices has been a recurring theme. Understanding the legal and moral boundaries of ethical hacking, coupled with the broader implications of responsible cybersecurity, positions you as a steward of digital integrity.

Crafting Your Secure and Ethical Digital Legacy

1. **Continuous Learning and Adaptation:** The digital landscape is ever-changing, and your commitment to continuous learning is the key to staying ahead. Embrace new technologies, stay informed about emerging threats, and evolve your skills to remain at the forefront of cybersecurity.

2. **Application of Knowledge:** The knowledge gained from the TOR Blueprint is not static; it is a dynamic force that can shape your digital legacy. Apply your skills responsibly, whether it's navigating the deep web securely, conducting ethical hacking practices, or implementing advanced security strategies.

3. **Influence on Others:** As you navigate the digital realm with wisdom and ethical clarity, your actions

ripple through the broader cybersecurity community. Share your knowledge, mentor others, and contribute to a culture of responsible cybersecurity practices. Your influence can shape the ethical conduct of those around you.

4. **Legacy of Responsibility:** Craft a legacy founded on responsibility and integrity. Uphold ethical standards, respect legal boundaries, and consider the broader moral implications of your actions. Your commitment to ethical excellence becomes an enduring aspect of your digital legacy.

Inspiring Future Generations

In conclusion, the TOR Blueprint journey extends beyond individual mastery; it extends to the inspiration of future generations. As you apply your knowledge to create a secure and ethical digital legacy, inspire others to follow suit. Foster a community where responsible cybersecurity practices are the norm, and where each individual contributes to the collective effort of crafting a trustworthy digital future.

Remember, your digital legacy is not merely a reflection of your technical prowess; it is a testament to your commitment to ethical conduct, continuous learning, and the responsible stewardship of the digital landscape. Craft a legacy that resonates with integrity, empowers those around you, and contributes to a vibrant and secure digital ecosystem.

Embark on this journey with confidence, purpose, and a dedication to crafting a digital legacy that stands the test of time. The TOR Blueprint is not just a guide; it is a foundation upon which you can build a legacy of ethical cybersecurity excellence.

DARKNET

Expert Guide to Online Anonymity and Digital Secrecy

Dedication

To the curious souls who peek beyond the surface, To the daydreamers who build castles in code, To the everyday heroes whispering secrets in encrypted chats, This book is your secret handshake in the digital dance.

No matter if you're a seasoned shadow explorer or just taking your first steps, these pages hold your key to online freedom. They'll teach you tricks to vanish, tools to outsmart the trackers, and the confidence to own your digital destiny.

So grab your flashlight and dive into the hidden corners of the web. Together, we'll rewrite the rules and reclaim the shadows as our playground.

Remember, privacy isn't about hiding, it's about choosing how you shine. Go forth, light your spark, and let the shadows dance!

About the Author

Ryan Knight isn't your typical security expert. His expertise was forged not in boardrooms, but in the shadowy corners of the internet, where he honed his skills as a hacker and trainer for the FBI and NSA.

His passion for online anonymity isn't about secrecy for its own sake, but about empowering individuals to reclaim their digital sovereignty in an age of surveillance.

In "Darknet: Expert Guide to Online Anonymity and Digital Secrecy," Ryan invites you on a thrilling journey through the darknet's hidden pathways, arming you with the knowledge to protect your privacy, explore its potential, and navigate its challenges with confidence.

Join him. Unmask the secrets of the shadows, master the tools of anonymity, and reclaim your rightful place as a free and empowered citizen of the digital world.

CHAPTER 1: WHY PRIVACY MATTERS

Imagine a world where every whispered word, every fleeting thought, every click and keystroke is laid bare. Not just to the NSA or some faceless corporation, but to anyone – your neighbor, your boss, your ex. A world where privacy isn't a right, but a luxury reserved for the tech elite and the deeply paranoid. Welcome to the precipice of that world, to the edge of the looking glass into a future increasingly defined by a lack of privacy.

This isn't some dystopian novel; it's the reality we're sleepwalking into. Governments hungry for control collect our data without a blink, corporations monetize our every move, and hackers lurk in the shadows, ready to exploit any vulnerability. Our digital footprints paint an intimate portrait of who we are – our desires, our fears, our secrets – laid bare for anyone with the right tools or enough rubles.

But within this chilling reality lies a flicker of defiance, a rebellion against the panoptic gaze. It's called privacy, and in the labyrinthine underbelly of the internet, it has a name: the Darknet. It's a place where shadows dance and anonymity reigns, where you can shed your digital skin and step into a world free from the prying eyes of the state, the corporations, and the voyeurs.

So, why should you care about privacy? It's not just about hiding your browsing history from your mother-in-law (though that can be handy). It's about protecting your freedom of expression, your right to dissent, your very ability to be an individual in a world increasingly obsessed with categorization and control.

Imagine speaking your mind on a controversial topic without fear of reprisal. Imagine exploring unpopular ideas without being labeled an extremist. Imagine pursuing your passions, both online and offline, without your every move being tracked and monetized. This is the promise of privacy, the potential for a world where your thoughts and actions belong to you, and only you.

But to truly understand the importance of privacy, we need to understand the threats that loom.

The Ghost in the Machine: The Threats to Privacy

Governments: From mass surveillance programs to data retention laws, governments are increasingly turning into digital Big Brothers, watching our every move and collecting our most intimate information. The line between national security and individual liberty blurs ever finer, leaving citizens at the mercy of algorithms and opaque bureaucracies.

Corporations: Driven by the insatiable hunger for data, corporations mine our online lives for every nugget of information they can. Our browsing habits, our social media posts, our location data – it's all grist for the mill, turned into targeted advertising and manipulative algorithms. They know us better than we know ourselves, and they use that knowledge to influence our choices, sell us things we don't need, and manipulate our behavior.

Hackers: Lurking in the shadows of the digital world, hackers are the opportunistic predators of the online jungle. They exploit vulnerabilities in software and systems, steal our data, and hold it hostage for ransom. Our financial information, our medical records, our very identities – all are up for grabs in the hands of a skilled hacker.

Is there hope?

In the face of these threats, it's easy to fall into despair. But that's where the Darknet comes in. It's not a panacea, but it's a powerful tool for reclaiming your privacy, a weapon against the digital panopticon. In the following chapters, we'll delve into the intricacies of the Darknet, explore its tools and techniques, and equip you with the knowledge and skills to navigate this hidden world safely and effectively.

This is not just a book about technology; it's a call to action. It's a call to reclaim your right to privacy, to protect your freedom of expression, and to carve out a space in the digital world where you can be yourself, without fear or judgment.

CHAPTER 2: THE BUILDING BLOCKS OF ANONYMITY

In the last chapter, we explored the chilling reality of our shrinking digital privacy and the potential of the Darknet to fight back. Now, it's time to roll up our sleeves and learn the key tools we'll use to build our very own fortress of anonymity. Think of it like constructing a secret hideout, but instead of bricks and mortar, we'll use virtual building blocks like encryption, pseudonymity, and that legendary guardian of online shadows – Tor.

First Base: Encryption – Sealing the Secrets Away

Imagine sending a postcard written in a language only you and the recipient understand. That's essentially what encryption does with your data. It scrambles your information into a jumbled mess, like a locked treasure chest, using complex algorithms that require a special key to unlock. This key becomes the password to your digital secrets, ensuring only authorized eyes can decipher them.

Think of email or online banking. When you log in with a password, an encryption handshake happens, making sure your info travels securely between your device and the website. Pretty cool, right? But encryption comes in different flavors, each with its own strengths and quirks.

- Symmetric Encryption: Think of it as a single key for both locking and unlocking the treasure chest. It's efficient for quick exchanges, but if someone gets hold of that key, all your secrets are out in the open.

- Asymmetric Encryption: This is like having two keys – a public key everyone can see (like the lock on the chest) and a private key kept hidden under your mattress (the key to unlock it). You share the public key with anyone who needs to send you encrypted messages, but only you have the private key to decrypt them, making it much more secure.

Second Base: Pseudonymity – Wearing a Digital Mask

Imagine walking into a party with a cool alias and a killer disguise. Pseudonymity works the same way online. You shed your real name and use a fake one, like a pseudonym author using a pen name. This protects your real identity while still allowing you to interact online. Think of forums and online communities where you can choose a username and express yourself without revealing your full name.

But don't get too comfortable. While pseudonymity makes you harder to track, it's not foolproof. If you link your pseudonym to your real-world identity through emails or social media, your mask can slip.

The Big Gun: Tor – The Labyrinthine Defender

Now, picture yourself navigating a city through a network of secret tunnels and passageways, each one leading to another, making it impossible for anyone to track your path. That's Tor in a nutshell. It's a free software that bounces your internet traffic through multiple relays around the world, making it almost impossible to pinpoint your location or origin. Think of it as the ultimate shield against online snooping.

Tor is powerful, but like any tool, it's not perfect. It can be slower than regular browsing, and some websites might block it. But for serious anonymity seekers, Tor is a must-have in their privacy toolkit.

Building Your Privacy Toolkit: Mixing and Matching for Maximum Protection

Remember, the best defense is a layered one. Just like mixing spices enhances the flavor of a dish, combining different anonymity tools can significantly boost your online stealth. Here's a basic toolkit to get you started:

- A strong password manager: Generate and store unique passwords for each website you use, making it harder for hackers to crack a single password and access all your accounts.

- A privacy-focused browser: Consider options like Firefox and Brave that prioritize user privacy over data collection.

- Encryption software: Encrypt your sensitive files and folders to keep them safe from prying eyes even if your device is compromised.

- Tor: For venturing into the Darknet or when extra anonymity is needed.

Remember, your privacy toolkit is unique to you and your needs. As you gain confidence and knowledge, you can experiment and add more tools to your arsenal. Just keep in mind that while anonymity is powerful, it's not magic. Responsible online behavior and a healthy dose of paranoia are always your best allies.

Now, with these foundation blocks in place, we're ready to delve deeper into the fascinating world of the Darknet in the next chapter. Get ready to put on your digital cloak and hood – the adventure awaits!

Chapter 3: Tor: The King of Anonymity Networks

Tor, the king of anonymity networks, isn't a single entity, but a sprawling ecosystem buzzing with interconnected parts. Understanding how these elements work together is crucial for navigating this labyrinthine path to online privacy. So, grab your digital compass and join us as we delve into the fascinating world of the Tor ecosystem.

The Architects: Tor Relays - Pillars of the Labyrinth

Imagine a hidden network of relay stations, each one dedicated to obscuring your digital trail. These are the Tor relays, the lifeblood of the ecosystem. These volunteer-run computers receive your encrypted data, strip away a layer of encryption, and send it on to another random relay in the network. This multi-hop dance continues until your data reaches its final destination, effectively erasing your footprints along the way.

To visualize this, picture yourself sending a letter cloaked in multiple envelopes. Each relay removes one envelope, revealing an address for the next relay, further masking your original location. By the time the final envelope reaches its recipient, your trail is cold, your location shrouded in the vastness of the network.

Types of Tor Relays:

- Entry Guards: The first stop on your Tor journey, these relays act as trusted entry points into the network.

- Middle Relays: The backbone of the ecosystem, these relays handle the bulk of data traffic, forwarding it through the labyrinth.

- Exit Nodes: The final stop before your data reaches its destination, these relays are responsible for decrypting the last layer and sending it out into the clearnet (the regular internet).

Downloading and Setting Up Tor:

Ready to join the Tor ecosystem? The journey begins with the Tor Browser Bundle, available for download on their official website: https://www.torproject.org/download/. This bundle comes pre-configured with everything you need to navigate the Tor network, including the Tor Browser itself. Installation is straightforward, and getting started is as simple as launching the browser and connecting to the network.

Unmasking the Gatekeepers: Exit Nodes - The Final Frontier

After traversing the labyrinthine Tor network, your data reaches its final destination through an exit node. Think of it as the doorway back to the clearnet, the point where your data emerges from the shadows. While the relays have stripped away your identifying information, the exit node plays a crucial role in the anonymity equation.

Choosing Your Guardians Wisely:

The choice of exit node impacts your security and experience. Ideally, you want one that:

- Resides in a privacy-friendly jurisdiction: Choose nodes located in countries with strong data protection laws and minimal government surveillance.

- Has a good reputation: Opt for well-established nodes with reliable uptime and minimal malicious activity reported.

- Matches your needs: Some nodes may be optimized for speed, while others prioritize security or censorship circumvention. Choose based on your individual needs.

The Shadow Side of the Gateway:

Despite their importance, exit nodes pose a potential vulnerability. Since they decrypt the final layer of your data and send it to the clearnet, they have the technical capability to eavesdrop on your traffic. To mitigate this risk:

- Use HTTPS wherever possible: Encrypting your communication adds an extra layer of protection on top of Tor's anonymity.

- Be mindful of what you do on Tor: While Tor helps mask your identity, it doesn't make you invincible. Avoid sensitive activities like online banking or sharing confidential information on exit nodes.

The Price of Privacy: Risks and Limitations of Using Tor

Like any powerful tool, Tor comes with its own set of limitations and potential risks. Understanding these caveats is crucial for making informed decisions about your online anonymity journey.

Speed Bumps on the Labyrinthine Path:

Tor's multi-hop architecture naturally impacts your internet speed. Data takes longer to traverse the network, resulting in slower browsing and download times. Patience is key if you choose to embrace the Tor ecosystem.

Exit Node Vulnerability: As mentioned earlier, exit nodes pose a potential security risk. Choosing trustworthy nodes and practicing responsible online behavior are essential to minimizing this risk.

Government Scrutiny: The association of Tor with certain online activities attracts scrutiny from some governments. While not illegal in itself, be aware of potential restrictions or monitoring in your region.

Legal Gray Areas: Certain activities on Tor, like accessing illegal markets or engaging in hacking, are illegal. Remember, anonymity isn't a license to break the law.

Beyond the Technical Hurdles:

Using Tor can require a slight shift in your online habits. Websites may load slower, some may not work at all, and accessing certain services might be more challenging. But remember, the trade-off is increased privacy and online freedom.

Joining the Labyrinthine Community: Exploring the Tor Ecosystem

While the anonymity Tor offers can be a solitary journey, it's far from a lonely one. The Tor ecosystem boasts a vibrant and diverse community of individuals drawn together by a shared desire for online freedom and privacy. This community offers invaluable support, resources, and a sense of belonging for those navigating the labyrinthine paths of the network.

Forums and Hidden Wikis:

Dive into the bustling Tor forums, where users share tips, troubleshoot issues, and discuss the latest developments in the ecosystem. Hidden wikis, accessible only through Tor, offer a wealth of information on everything from choosing exit nodes to finding hidden services (websites accessible only through Tor).

Mailing Lists and IRC Channels:

Engage in real-time conversations on Tor-specific mailing lists and IRC channels. These platforms foster a sense of community, allowing you to connect with like-minded individuals, ask questions, and learn from experienced users.

Events and Conferences:

Venture beyond the digital realm and attend Tor-related conferences and workshops happening around the world. These events provide opportunities to network with fellow enthusiasts, learn from experts, and contribute to the ongoing development of the ecosystem.

Contributing to the Cause:

The Tor Project relies on the dedication of volunteers to maintain and improve the network. Whether it's offering technical expertise, translating documentation, or simply spreading awareness, there are numerous ways to contribute to the cause and strengthen the community.

Remember, the Tor ecosystem is more than just a network; it's a movement. It's a community of individuals united by a common goal: protecting online privacy and promoting digital freedom. By joining the conversation, sharing your knowledge, and contributing to the cause, you become an integral part of this movement, ensuring the continued existence of this vital labyrinth of anonymity for generations to come.

So, are you ready to take the plunge? Download the Tor Browser, explore the resources, and join the labyrinthine community. The journey towards online privacy awaits.

Additional Resources:

- Tor Project website: https://www.torproject.org/

- Tor Blog: https://blog.torproject.org/

- Tor Forum: https://forum.torproject.org/

- The Hidden Wiki: http://b7zq5i7zftu5y73pw.onion/

- Tor IRC channel: #tor on Libera.Chat

With this chapter concluded, we've shed light on the inner workings of the Tor network, its strengths and limitations, and the vibrant community that sustains it. Remember, the journey to online privacy is a continuous one, and the Tor ecosystem offers a powerful tool for navigating the labyrinthine paths towards a more secure and free internet. Now, with knowledge as your guide and community at your side, venture forth and explore the depths of the Darknet, always remembering to tread cautiously and responsibly.

CHAPTER 4: BEYOND TOR: ALTERNATIVE ANONYMITY NETWORKS

While Tor reigns supreme as the king of anonymity networks, its labyrinthine paths aren't for everyone. In this chapter, we'll set sail for uncharted waters and explore alternative anonymity networks like I2P and Zcash, each offering unique features and trade-offs. So, fasten your digital life vests and prepare to dive into the depths of online privacy beyond the Tor horizon.

I2P: Building Your Own Island of Anonymity

Imagine not just navigating a labyrinth, but building your own hidden island within it. That's the essence of I2P (Invisible Internet Project), a peer-to-peer network where users directly connect with each other, eliminating the need for centralized servers. This unique architecture offers several advantages:

- Enhanced Security: With no central points of failure, I2P is inherently more resistant to attack and surveillance.

- Greater Control: Users have significant control over their anonymity, customizing their connections and network settings.

- Censorship Resistance: I2P is highly resistant to censorship and blocking attempts, making it a valuable tool in restrictive environments.

However, this island paradise comes with its own quirks:

- Steeper Learning Curve: Setting up and using I2P can be technically demanding, requiring more effort than the user-friendly Tor Browser.

- Slower Network: The peer-to-peer nature of I2P typically leads to slower speeds compared to Tor, making it less suitable for bandwidth-intensive activities.

- Limited Ecosystem: The I2P network is smaller than Tor, offering a narrower range of applications and services.

Zcash: Cloaking Your Coins in Secrecy

While Tor hides your online footprints, it doesn't mask your financial transactions. Enter Zcash, a privacy-focused cryptocurrency leveraging cutting-edge cryptography to shield your financial movements from prying eyes. Zcash boasts several unique features:

- Selective Transparency: Transactions can be either transparent or shielded, offering flexibility and control over your privacy needs.

- Enhanced Fungibility: All Zcash coins are indistinguishable, preventing tracking and analysis of individual transactions.

- Stronger Security: Zcash utilizes advanced cryptographic techniques, making it resistant to sophisticated hacking attempts.

However, the shiny Zcash coin also has its tarnished corners:

- Complexity and Uncertainty: Zcash's underlying cryptography is complex and not fully understood, raising concerns about potential vulnerabilities.

- Regulatory Scrutiny: As a privacy-focused cryptocurrency, Zcash attracts scrutiny from governments and financial institutions, potentially limiting its widespread adoption.

- Limited Integration: Compared to more established cryptocurrencies, Zcash has a smaller merchant and exchange network, reducing its practical use cases.

Choosing the Right Network: Mapping Your Anonymity Journey

So, which network should you choose? The answer, like all things in life, depends on your individual needs and priorities. Here's a handy compass to guide you:

- For the Privacy Purist: If anonymity is your paramount concern, and you're comfortable with technical complexity, I2P's decentralized architecture might be your haven.

- For the Tech-Savvy Financier: If financial privacy is your primary goal, and you're willing to navigate the uncharted waters of cryptography, Zcash could be your digital fortress.

- For the Everyday User: For most users seeking robust anonymity without deep technical dives, Tor remains the tried-and-true option, offering user-friendliness and a vibrant ecosystem.

Remember, the perfect anonymity network doesn't exist. Each option comes with its own set of strengths and weaknesses, making it crucial to understand your needs and choose the tool that best aligns with your personal digital journey. Explore, experiment, and stay informed! With knowledge as your compass and caution as your rudder, you can navigate the diverse seas of anonymity, charting your own course towards a more private and secure digital future.

Here are links and steps to get started with each of the anonymity networks discussed:

I2P

- Official Website: https://geti2p.net/en/

- Getting Started
  Guide: https://geti2p.net/en/download

- Key Steps:

  1. Download and install the I2P software from the official website.

  2. Run the I2P router application.

  3. Configure your web browser to use I2P (instructions provided in the getting started guide).

  4. Access I2P-specific websites and services through your configured browser.

Zcash

- Official Website: https://z.cash/

- Getting Started Guide: https://z.cash/get-started/

- Key Steps:

    1. Create a Zcash wallet (either a standalone wallet or one integrated with an exchange).

    2. Obtain Zcash coins through exchange platforms or mining.

    3. Use your wallet to send and receive Zcash privately.

Tor

- Official Website: https://www.torproject.org/

- Download Tor Browser: https://www.torproject.org/download/

- Key Steps:

    1. Download and install the Tor Browser Bundle from the official website.

    2. Run the Tor Browser.

3. Access websites through the Tor network by simply browsing as you normally would.

Additional Tips for Using Anonymity Networks:

- Stay informed: Keep up-to-date with the latest news and developments related to each network.

- Use reputable services: Only access websites and services that are known to be trustworthy and secure.

- Practice good security hygiene: Use strong passwords, enable two-factor authentication, and be cautious about the information you share online.

- Respect the law: Remember that anonymity networks do not exempt you from legal obligations. Use them responsibly and ethically.

This chapter concludes our exploration of the captivating world of anonymity networks. We've ventured beyond the familiar shores of Tor, discovering the unique landscapes of I2P and Zcash, and equipped you with the tools to choose the network that best fits your needs. Remember, the quest for online privacy is an ongoing adventure, and the diverse tools at your disposal empower you to reclaim your digital freedom, one anonymous step at a time.

Chapter 5: Securing Your Communications

Email, Messaging, and More

In the digital age, every message you send, every call you make, leaves a trail in the ether. But fear not, privacy warrior! This chapter equips you with the tools and tactics to turn your communications into hushed whispers, shielding them from prying ears and curious eyes. We'll dive into anonymizing your email, instant messaging, and even phone calls, weaving your own cloak of digital secrecy.

Email: From Open Postcards to Encrypted Missives

Imagine sending your emails not on flimsy postcards, but in locked metal boxes, delivered by trusted couriers. That's essentially what encrypted email does. Here are your options:

- End-to-End Encryption (E2EE) Services: Services like ProtonMail, Tutanota, and StartMail offer E2EE for your emails, ensuring only the sender and recipient can access the content.

- PGP (Pretty Good Privacy) Encryption: For the tech-savvy, PGP provides another layer of encryption, allowing you to secure emails sent to any recipient, even those not using E2EE services.

Instant Messaging: From Public Square to Hidden Alleyways

Leaving your conversations exposed in public squares like Facebook Messenger or WhatsApp isn't ideal. Fortunately, there are more secluded alleyways of the digital world:

- Signal: This widely used app boasts E2EE messaging, disappearing messages, and screenshot blocking, making it a haven for confidential chats.

- Telegram: While not E2EE by default, Telegram's "Secret Chats" offer E2EE and self-destructing messages, ideal for sensitive conversations.

- Wickr Me: This ephemeral messaging app disappears messages after a set time, ensuring complete privacy and zero digital footprints.

Phone Calls: From Open Lines to Encrypted Tunnels

- Signal Private Messenger: Not just for messaging, Signal also offers secure voice calls with E2EE encryption.

- Silent Circle: This subscription-based service provides E2EE voice calls, messaging, and video conferencing for business-level security.

- Jitsi Meet: For open-source enthusiasts, Jitsi Meet offers browser-based, E2EE-encrypted video conferencing without the need for downloads or installations.

Best Practices for Secure Communication:

Now that you have your digital cloak and dagger, here are some essential practices to maintain your communication security:

- Choose strong passwords and enable two-factor authentication (2FA) for all your accounts.

- Be cautious about what information you share online, especially with unfamiliar individuals.

- Avoid using public Wi-Fi for sensitive communication.

- Remember, no security is foolproof. Be vigilant and adapt your techniques based on your threat level.

Embracing a Culture of Privacy

Securing your communication isn't just about shielding individual messages; it's about cultivating a culture of privacy in your digital life. By taking conscious steps to control your data and safeguard your conversations, you reclaim your right to a private space in the online world. Remember, your whispers deserve to be heard only by those you choose, not the digital eavesdroppers lurking in the shadows.

With this chapter, we've demystified the world of secure communication, equipping you with the tools and tactics to cloak your words in a shroud of digital secrecy. As you navigate the ever-evolving landscape of online privacy, remember that your dedication to secure communication is a small flame flickering against the darkness, paving the way for a future where whispers can carry freely, unburdened by fear and unfettered by intrusive eyes. Keep whispering, dear reader, and together we'll make sure our voices are heard, loud and clear, within the hushed chambers of digital privacy.

This concludes our exploration of the essential tools and techniques for navigating the Darknet and beyond. From understanding hidden networks to securing your communications, you're now equipped to venture deeper into the labyrinthine alleys of online anonymity, safeguarding your freedom and privacy in the digital age. Remember, knowledge is your shield, caution is your compass, and responsibility is your torch. Embrace the shadows, wield your tools wisely, and keep exploring the hidden corners of the internet where your true voice can still be heard.

CHAPTER 6: BROWSING THE WEB ANONYMOUSLY

Surfing the web, once a carefree joyride, has become a minefield of trackers, surveillance, and targeted ads. But fear not, digital pirates! This chapter equips you with the tools and tactics to navigate the stormy seas of online anonymity, becoming a ghost ship gliding unseen under the digital radar. We'll dive into the two main anchors of anonymous browsing – Tor and VPNs – exploring their strengths, weaknesses, and how to choose the right one for your unique needs.

Tor: The Labyrinthine Cloak of Anonymity

Imagine your internet traffic meandering through a maze of encrypted tunnels, bouncing off countless relays before reaching its destination. That's the magic of Tor, the anonymity network weaving a cloak of obscurity around your browsing habits. Here's what it offers:

- Strong Anonymity: Tor's multi-hop architecture makes it incredibly difficult to track your online movements, keeping your browsing history and location shrouded in secrecy.

- Censorship Circumvention: Tor bypasses geographical restrictions and firewalls, letting you access blocked websites and information freely.

- Privacy Protection: Tor shields your data from snoopers, prying eyes, and malicious actors, safeguarding your online identity.

But even the Labyrinthine King has its limitations:

- Speed Bumps: The multi-hop journey comes at a cost – slower internet speeds are the price for your digital invisibility.

- Exit Node Vulnerability: While your data is encrypted within the Tor network, the final exit node can potentially see your unencrypted traffic.

- Technical Complexity: Setting up and using Tor requires more technical expertise than using a simple browser.

VPNs: Tunneling Through the Digital Landscape

Imagine yourself driving through a secure tunnel, shielded from prying eyes on the open road. That's essentially what a VPN (Virtual Private Network) does – it encrypts your internet traffic and routes it through a remote server, masking your true location and identity. Here are its benefits:

- Location Masking: VPNs change your virtual location, letting you access geo-restricted content and bypass censorship.

- Enhanced Security: Encryption protects your data from prying eyes on public Wi-Fi networks and untrusted connections.

- Privacy Boost: VPNs hide your IP address, making it harder for websites and online services to track your online activity.

However, the VPN tunnel also has its tollbooths:

- Subscription Costs: Most reliable VPNs require paid subscriptions, adding a financial cost to your anonymity.

- Performance Impact: Depending on the server location and your internet connection, VPNs can also slow down your internet speed.

- Trust Factor: Choosing a trustworthy VPN provider is crucial, as they handle your encrypted data.

Choosing Your Vessel: Tor vs. VPN – A Captain's Dilemma

So, which digital vessel should you set sail with? The answer, like most things in life, depends on your needs and priorities:

- For Ultimate Anonymity: Tor reigns supreme, especially for bypassing censorship and protecting against advanced tracking.

- For Convenience and Location Masking: VPNs offer ease of use and location flexibility, ideal for everyday browsing and accessing geo-restricted content.

- For a Balanced Approach: Combining Tor with a VPN provides ultimate security, but at the cost of slower speeds and technical complexity.

Remember, no single tool is perfect. Assess your threat level, browsing habits, and technical aptitude to choose the right balance of anonymity and convenience.

Beyond the Tools: Sailing With Caution

Regardless of your chosen vessel, remember:

- Choose trustworthy tools: Do your research and select reputable Tor relays and VPN providers.

- Practice good online hygiene: Use strong passwords, avoid suspicious websites, and be mindful of the information you share online.

- Stay informed: Keep up-to-date with the latest developments in the world of online privacy and security.

Embracing the Ghostly Life

Browsing anonymously isn't just about hiding your online tracks; it's about reclaiming your digital freedom. By wielding the tools and tactics in this chapter, you transform from a tracked and targeted user into a digital ghost, invisible to the prying eyes of the online world. So, raise your anonymized sails, captain, and chart your course toward a more private and secure internet experience. Remember, the open seas beckon, and the shadows of the digital labyrinth wait for you to explore their hidden depths.

This concludes our exploration of the essential tools and tactics for navigating the Darknet and beyond. From understanding hidden networks to securing your communications and browsing anonymously, you're now equipped to venture deeper into the labyrinthine alleys of online anonymity, safeguarding your freedom and privacy in the digital age. Remember, knowledge is your shield, caution is your compass.

Here are some links to get started with the tools and resources discussed in Chapter 6:

Tor:

- Official Website: https://www.torproject.org/

- Download Tor
  Browser: https://www.torproject.org/download/

- Tor Documentation: https://tb-manual.torproject.org/

VPNs:

- Independent VPN Review Sites:

  - https://www.trustpilot.com/review/vpnmentor.com

  - https://www.top10vpn.com/

  - https://www.privacyguides.org/en/basics/vpn-overview/

- Popular VPN Providers:

  - NordVPN: https://nordvpn.com/

  - ExpressVPN: https://www.expressvpn.com/

- ○ ProtonVPN: https://protonvpn.com/

Additional Resources:

- Electronic Frontier Foundation (EFF): https://www.eff.org/

- Privacy International: https://privacyinternational.org/

- Digital Shadows: https://www.reliaquest.com/platform/digital-risk-protection/

Choosing the Right Tool:

- Tor vs. VPN Comparison Chart: https://www.elite-proxy.net/vpn-vs-tor-whats-the-difference-for-online-privacy-and-anonymity/

- Privacy Tools & Services Directory: https://www.privacytools.io/

Remember, the best approach to online anonymity often involves combining multiple tools and techniques. Research your options, choose what works best for your needs, and stay vigilant about your online security practices.

I hope these resources help you navigate the shadows of the digital sea with confidence!

CHAPTER 7: ANONYMITY ON THE GO

Mobile Devices and Tor

The digital revolution has placed the internet in our pockets, but with it comes the constant shadow of surveillance and data collection. But fear not, intrepid mobile voyagers! This chapter equips you with the tools and tactics to transform your smartphone into a phantom vessel, sailing the seas of online anonymity while leaving barely a ripple in your wake. We'll dive into the challenges and solutions for using Tor and other anonymity tools on your mobile devices, empowering you to reclaim your digital freedom on the go.

Tor in Your Pocket: Weaving a Mobile Web of Secrecy

The mighty Tor Browser isn't confined to desktops; it boasts mobile versions for both Android and iOS, letting you cloak your mobile browsing in its labyrinthine layers of anonymity. Here's what you need to know:

- Tor Browser for Android: The official and recommended option, offering strong anonymity and a familiar Tor experience.

- Onion Browser for iOS: Due to Apple's restrictions, Onion Browser relies on iOS's built-in web engine, limiting Tor's full features but still providing basic anonymity.

Navigating the Mobile Labyrinth: Challenges and Solutions

While Tor unlocks mobile anonymity, the path isn't without its bumps:

- Battery Drain: Tor's multi-hop connections can significantly drain your battery, necessitating a portable charger if venturing far from an outlet.

- Performance Impact: Expect slower browsing speeds when using Tor on mobile, especially compared to your usual data connection.

- Limited Ecosystem: Not all websites or apps are accessible through Tor on mobile, requiring extra caution and potentially limiting your options.

Overcoming the Obstacles: Tips for Mobile Anonymity

Embrace these tactics to smooth your anonymous mobile journey:

- Pre-download essential resources: Save offline copies of crucial websites or documents to minimize reliance on live Tor browsing.

- Utilize Wi-Fi for heavier tasks: Reserve bandwidth-intensive activities like streaming or video calls for regular internet connections.

- Stay informed: Keep up-to-date with the latest Tor mobile developments and adjust your tactics accordingly.

Beyond Tor: Additional Mobile Anonymity Tools

While Tor stands tall, your mobile anonymity arsenal can benefit from other tools:

- VPNs: Offer location masking and additional encryption, but can be resource-intensive and often require subscriptions.

- Privacy-focused Browsers: Alternatives like DuckDuckGo and Firefox Focus offer basic privacy features without the full Tor experience.

- Messaging Apps: Signal and Telegram provide secure messaging with additional privacy features like disappearing messages.

Embracing the Mobile Ghost: A Call to Action

Mobile anonymity isn't just about technical tricks; it's a mindset shift. Be mindful of the information you share on your phone, practice good app hygiene, and remember that true anonymity requires vigilance and responsible digital habits.

With the tools and tips in this chapter, you're now equipped to transform your mobile device from a surveillance tool into a vessel of digital freedom. So, raise your anonymized sails, intrepid voyager, and chart your course towards a more private and secure mobile experience. Remember, the road less traveled, shrouded in the shadows of anonymity, awaits your exploration.

From understanding hidden networks to securing your communications and browsing anonymously, you're now empowered to reclaim your digital freedom and privacy in the ever-evolving landscape of the online world. Remember, knowledge is your shield, caution is your compass, and responsibility is your torch. Embrace the shadows, wield your tools wisely, and continue your exploration of the hidden corners of the internet where your true voice can still be heard, loud and clear, within the hushed chambers of digital privacy.

Now, go forth and explore with confidence, leaving only the faintest footprints in the sands of cyberspace. The Darknet, with all its potential and perils, awaits.

Chapter 8: Encryption: The Ultimate Shield

In a world where information is currency, encryption stands as the ultimate shield, guarding your secrets against prying eyes and malicious forces. This chapter delves into the art of digital alchemy, revealing how encryption transforms ordinary data into unintelligible ciphers, protecting your privacy and securing your communications. We'll explore the inner workings of encryption, unravel the mysteries of different algorithms, and equip you with the knowledge to forge your own impenetrable fortress in the digital realm.

The Magical Cipher: Transforming Data into Puzzles

Imagine a language so intricate, so complex, that only those with the right key can decipher its meaning. That's the essence of encryption. It takes your sensitive data—messages, files, passwords—and scrambles it using mathematical algorithms, rendering it unreadable to anyone without the decryption key.

The Key Keepers: Symmetric and Asymmetric Encryption

Encryption's magic relies on two distinct guardians of the keys:

- Symmetric Encryption: Like a secret handshake, both parties use the same key to encrypt and decrypt data. It's fast and efficient, but sharing the key securely can be challenging.

    - Common Algorithms: AES (Advanced Encryption Standard), Blowfish, Twofish.

- Asymmetric Encryption: A dance of two keys—a public key shared openly, and a private key kept hidden. Anyone can encrypt with the public key, but only the holder of the private key can decrypt, ensuring secure communication without prior key exchange.

    - Common Algorithms: RSA (Rivest-Shamir-Adleman), ECC (Elliptic Curve Cryptography).

Strength in Diversity: Cipher Suites and Hashing

Encryption's power grows when combined with other techniques:

- Cipher Suites: Bundles of algorithms and protocols working in harmony to secure different aspects of communication, ensuring
confidentiality, integrity, and authentication.

- Hashing: A one-way encryption that creates unique fingerprints of data, used for password storage, file integrity checks, and digital signatures.

  - Common Hashing Algorithms: SHA-256, SHA-3, MD5.

Choosing Your Armor: Strengths and Weaknesses of Algorithms

Each algorithm has its unique strengths and potential vulnerabilities:

- AES: The gold standard for symmetric encryption, known for its speed and resilience against attacks.

- RSA: A widely used asymmetric algorithm, but its security depends on key length and proper implementation.

- ECC: A newer asymmetric algorithm offering stronger security with smaller keys, making it ideal for resource-constrained devices.

Beyond the Technical: Encryption in Action

Encryption isn't just for spies and hackers; it's woven into the fabric of our digital lives:

- Securing Online Transactions: HTTPS protects your financial data and passwords when shopping or banking online.

- Protecting Personal Communications: Secure messaging apps like Signal and WhatsApp employ end-to-end encryption to safeguard your conversations.

- Safeguarding Data Storage: Encrypting files and devices protects sensitive information from unauthorized access.

Wielding the Cipher: Tips for Everyday Encryption

Here are ways to integrate encryption into your digital life:

- Use password managers: Store and manage passwords securely with tools like LastPass or 1Password.

- Enable encryption on devices: Protect your smartphones and laptops with encryption features.

- Choose encrypted messaging apps: Opt for apps with strong encryption protocols for communication.

- Encrypt sensitive files: Use tools like VeraCrypt or PGP to protect important documents.

- Be mindful of key management: Protect your decryption keys securely, as losing them means losing access to your encrypted data.

Embracing the Cipher's Power: A Call to Action

In a world increasingly reliant on data, encryption is not a luxury; it's a necessity. By understanding its fundamentals and applying its tools wisely, you can forge a fortress of privacy and security in the digital realm. Remember, knowledge is your shield, and encryption is your sword. Wield them both with care, and navigate the digital landscape with confidence, knowing that your secrets are safe within the embrace of the cipher.

CHAPTER 9: COIN MIXING

Breaking the Trace

Welcome, fellow crypto enthusiast, to the labyrinthine world of coin mixing! In this chapter, we'll unravel the mysteries of this powerful tool used to anonymize cryptocurrency transactions, shedding light on its workings and empowering you to make informed decisions about its use.

The Problem: Transparent Trails on the Blockchain

Imagine every step you take with your cryptocurrency etched in stone, visible to anyone with a magnifying glass. That's the inherent transparency of the blockchain, offering security but sacrificing anonymity. Every transaction, from sender to receiver and beyond, is laid bare for all to see. This exposes users to potential risks like:

- Tracking and Surveillance: Your spending habits and financial connections can be analyzed by anyone, raising privacy concerns.

- Targeted Attacks: Hackers or malicious actors could potentially target your crypto holdings based on your transaction history.

- Price Manipulation: Large transactions can become visible, potentially influencing market prices and affecting your trades.

Enter the Coin Mixer: Breaking the Chains of Transparency

Coin mixing, also known as crypto tumbling, works like a magical laundry machine for your dirty crypto coins. It takes your crypto, throws it into a swirling pool with other users' coins, and then distributes a clean (and hopefully untraceable) portion back to you. Here's a simplified breakdown:

1. Deposit your coins: You send your cryptocurrency to a mixing service.

2. Coin Pool Formation: The service combines your coins with those from other users, creating a large pool.

3. Mixing Magic: The service employs various techniques to shuffle and anonymize the coins within the pool. Common methods include:

   o Chain splitting: Breaking down coins into smaller denominations and sending them through different paths on the blockchain.

- Coin swapping: Exchanging coins between pool participants, obscuring the original transaction trail.

- Delayed transactions: Scheduling payouts at random intervals to further break the link between deposits and withdrawals.

4. Withdrawal: You receive your "clean" coins back (minus a mixing fee) from a different address, ideally with no link back to your original deposit.

Unmasking the Risks and Limitations: Before You Take the Plunge

While coin mixing offers substantial anonymity benefits, it's crucial to understand its limitations and potential risks:

- Not Foolproof: Mixing services can't guarantee complete anonymity. Advanced blockchain analysis techniques might still trace some connections.

- Centralization Concerns: Relying on a third-party mixing service introduces trust issues. Choose reputable services with strong security practices.

- Transaction Delays: Mixing processes can take time, leading to delayed withdrawals and potential inconvenience.

- Legality Issues: Some jurisdictions view coin mixing with suspicion due to its association with illegal activities. Research local regulations before engaging in such services.

Taking the First Steps: A Beginner's Guide to Coin Mixing

If you're intrigued by the potential of coin mixing, here are some helpful starting points:

- Research mixing services: Look for reputable services with good reviews and strong security protocols. Check features like supported currencies, mixing algorithms, and fees.

- Start small: Don't jump into mixing large amounts right away. Experiment with small transactions to understand the process and assess the service's effectiveness.

- Practice caution: Use a secure VPN to mask your internet activity and always choose reliable wallets for storing your mixed coins.

- Stay informed: Keep up with the latest developments in blockchain analysis and privacy techniques to understand evolving risks and adjust your approach accordingly.

Beyond the Mix: A Call to Responsible Digital Citizenship

Coin mixing is a powerful tool, but it's not a magic bullet for absolute anonymity. Remember, responsible digital citizenship requires a holistic approach to privacy and security. Combine mixing with other best practices like secure password management, strong encryption, and mindful online behavior to maximize your anonymity and safeguard your crypto holdings.

Here are some helpful resources to expand on the information in Chapter 9:

Coin Mixing Services:

- Wasabi Wallet: https://cryptobriefing.com/wasabis-bitcoin-mixer-to-start-censoring-transactions/ (Provides detailed information about coin mixing and offers a user-friendly wallet with built-in mixing functionalities.)

- Blender.io: https://blendor.io/ (A popular mixing service with a focus on transparency and detailed statistics.)

- CoinJoin: https://blog.wasabiwallet.io/what-is-a-coinjoin/ (An open-source coin mixing software that allows users to mix their coins directly, without relying on a third-party service.)

Step-by-step Guides:

- How to Use Wasabi
  Wallet: https://cryptobriefing.com/wasabis-bitcoin-mixer-to-start-censoring-transactions/ (A comprehensive guide explaining how to use Wasabi Wallet for mixing Bitcoin.)

- Coin Mixing for
  Beginners: https://news.bitcoin.com/tumbling-bitcoins-guide-rinse-cycle/ (Provides a basic overview of coin mixing and walks you through the process using a specific service.)

- Understanding Coin
  Mixing: https://medium.com/thedarkside/top-10-bitcoin-mixers-and-bitcoin-tumbler-services-review-2020-1524445bf86d (Offers a technical explanation of the different coin mixing algorithms and their effectiveness.)

Additional Resources:

- Bitcoin
  Magazine: https://bitcoinmagazine.com/ (Provides news and information about Bitcoin and other cryptocurrencies, including articles on coin mixing and privacy.)

- Privacy Tools & Services
  Directory: https://www.privacytools.io/ (A
  comprehensive directory of tools and resources for
  online privacy, including coin mixing services.)

- Electronic Frontier Foundation
  (EFF): https://www.eff.org/ (Provides information
  and resources on internet privacy and digital
  rights, including the use of encryption and anonymity
  tools.)

Important Note:

Before using any coin mixing service, it's crucial to research them thoroughly. Consider factors like their reputation, security practices, supported currencies, fees, and potential legal implications in your jurisdiction. Remember, coin mixing is not a guarantee of complete anonymity, and it's essential to use it responsibly and with caution.

By using these resources and practicing responsible digital citizenship, you can gain a deeper understanding of coin mixing and make informed decisions about whether it's the right tool for your needs.

Embrace the knowledge you've gained in this chapter, and venture into the world of coin mixing with caution and understanding. Remember, anonymity is a journey, not a destination. Continue exploring, learning, and evolving your digital hygiene practices to navigate the blockchain with confidence and control, leaving only the faintest footprints in your wake.

Now go forth, mix with mindful wisdom, and enjoy the enhanced privacy and security that awaits!

CHAPTER 10: ANONYMITY FOR THE TRULY PARANOID

Welcome, fellow traveler in the labyrinthine alleys of digital anonymity. This chapter delves into the deepest shadows, catering to those whose pursuit of privacy transcends ordinary measures. We journey into the realm of advanced anonymity techniques, reserved for those with a heightened level of paranoia and a thirst for the most impregnable digital cloaks. Prepare to encounter intricate enclaves, enigmatic proofs, and a kaleidoscope of tools designed to vanish you utterly from the prying eyes of the cybernetic panopticon.

Fortress of Solitude: Secure Enclaves for the Impenetrable

Imagine a digital sanctuary, a space carved from the bedrock of the internet, accessible only through layers of impenetrable encryption and guarded by vigilant sentinels. Such is the domain of secure enclaves, fortified environments where you can conduct your digital machinations unseen, unheard, and untraceable. These havens utilize a cocktail of technologies, including:

- Hardware enclaves: Secure chips embedded within your device, acting as isolated fortresses for sensitive operations. Think of them as miniature, inviolable vaults within your digital walls.

- Trusted Execution Environments (TEEs): Secure virtualized spaces within your operating system, shielding your activities from the prying eyes of the main system. Imagine a hidden room within your digital house, accessible only through a secret passage.

- Secure multi-party computation (MPC): A collaborative approach where computations are distributed among multiple servers, with individual parties contributing only their inputs without ever having access to the complete picture. Think of a puzzle solved by blindfolded participants, each holding a piece, with the final image revealed only to the collective effort.

Beyond the Veil: Zero-Knowledge Proofs for Invisible Transactions

Imagine proving you know something without revealing what it is. That's the magic of zero-knowledge proofs, cryptographic tools that allow you to verify an assertion (say, owning a certain asset) without disclosing any identifying information. Think of it as unlocking a door by demonstrating your knowledge of the combination without anyone ever seeing the numbers themselves. These ethereal proofs serve as digital passports, granting access to services and resources without leaving a trace of your identity.

Navigating the Labyrinth: Tools for the Advanced Paranoid

Your toolbox for hyper-anonymity extends far beyond the usual suspects. Here are some potent tools for the truly cautious:

- Tails/Whonix: Specialized operating systems designed for anonymity and security, with features like Tor integration and persistent amnesiac browsing.

- Verifiable Random Functions (VRFs): Tools that generate unpredictable, verifiable randomness, ideal for anonymizing your interactions with blockchain networks.

- Homomorphic encryption: Allows computations to be performed on encrypted data without decryption, preserving privacy while utilizing data's full potential. Imagine a locked box where calculations happen inside, revealing only the results, not the contents.

- Secure multi-party communication (MPC): Enables confidential communication between multiple parties without any individual party having access to the entire conversation. Think of a group chat where everyone whispers, and only the collective meaning emerges.

A Call to Measured Paranoia: Security without Sacrifice

While your paranoia may be justified in these hyper-connected times, remember that absolute anonymity comes at a cost. Consider these trade-offs:

- Complexity: Advanced tools often require technical expertise and specialized knowledge, creating a steep learning curve.

- Availability: Some technologies are still in their infancy, offering limited functionality or compatibility.

- Convenience: Sacrificing ease of use and speed for enhanced anonymity can impact your daily workflow.

Embrace a measured paranoia, choosing solutions that strike the right balance between security and practicality. Layer your defenses strategically, prioritizing the threats you face most acutely. Remember, knowledge is your shield, and vigilance is your compass. Use them wisely as you navigate the shadowy alleys of this chapter, emerging equipped to vanish into the digital ether, a ghost amidst the machines.

This concludes our comprehensive exploration of anonymity in the digital age. From understanding hidden networks to securing your communications and employing advanced techniques, you are now empowered to reclaim your privacy and navigate the online world with confidence. Remember, knowledge is your shield, caution is your compass, and responsibility is your torch. Embrace the shadows, wield your tools with wisdom, and continue your exploration of the hidden corners of the internet where your true voice can still be heard, loud and clear, within the hushed chambers of digital privacy.

Now, go forth, vanish into the ether, and leave only the faintest whispers in your wake. The shadows await, and the truly paranoid shall always find their way.

To further enhance your exploration of advanced anonymity techniques, here are some helpful resources for each section of Chapter 10:

Secure Enclaves:

- Intel SGX: https://www.intel.com/content/www/us/en/download/19085/intel-software-guard-extensions-intel-sgx-driver-for-windows.html (Official Intel SGX website, with technical details and resources)

- AMD SEV: https://www.amd.com/en/developer/sev.html (Official AMD SEV website, with technical details and resources)

- Trusted Execution Environment (TEE) Alliance: https://www.securetechalliance.org/wp-content/uploads/TEE-101-White-Paper-V1.1-FINAL-June-2018.pdf (Industry consortium promoting TEE adoption, with educational resources and member companies)

Zero-Knowledge Proofs:

- Zero-Knowledge Proofs 101: https://crypto.stanford.edu/cs355/18sp/lec3.pdf (Stanford Computer Science Department's introductory article on ZKPs)

- Zcash: https://z.cash/ (Privacy-focused cryptocurrency utilizing ZKPs)

- zkSNARKs: https://blog.ethereum.org/2016/12/05/zksnarks-in-a-nutshell (Open-source library for building and verifying zkSNARK proofs)

Advanced Paranoia Toolbox:

- Tails: https://tails.net/support/faq/index.en.html (A mnesiac Linux distribution for secure browsing and anonymity)

- Whonix: https://www.whonix.org/ (Virtual machine distribution focused on online anonymity and security)

- Verifiable Random Functions (VRFs): https://en.wikipedia.org/wiki/Verifiable_ran dom_function (Wikipedia article on VRFs, with technical details and research papers)

- Homomorphic Encryption: https://en.wikipedia.org/wiki/Homomor phic_encryption (Wikipedia article on homomorphic encryption, with technical details and examples)

- Secure Multi-Party Computation (MPC): https://en.wikipedia.org/wiki/Secure_multi- party_computation (Wikipedia article on MPC, with technical details and research papers)

Additional Resources:

- The Privacy Tools & Services Directory: https://www.privacytools.io/ (Comprehensive directory of tools and resources for online privacy)

- The Electronic Frontier Foundation (EFF): https://www.eff.org/ (Non-profit organization promoting digital rights and privacy, with resources and research)

- Books:

  - "The Paranoiac's Guide to Hiding" by Edward Snowden and Bruce Schneier

  - "Zero-Knowledge Proofs: An Introduction" by Ariel Rubinstein and Asaf Rabinowitz

Remember: Implementing advanced anonymity techniques often requires technical expertise and careful consideration of trade-offs. Use these resources responsibly and prioritize solutions that align with your specific needs and threat landscape.

I hope these links provide a valuable starting point for your continued journey into the shadows!

CHAPTER 11: THE BATTLE FOR PRIVACY: GOVERNMENTS VS. BIG TECH

Welcome to the battleground of the 21st century - the battleground for privacy. In this arena, two titans clash: governments, wielding the sword of public safety and national security, and Big Tech, armed with the potent arsenal of data and innovation. This chapter delves into the heart of this ongoing conflict, exploring its origins, consequences, and the potential game-changers on the horizon, like blockchain and artificial intelligence.

The Genesis of the Clash: A Landscape of Data Collection

Our digital lives generate a constant stream of data - our every click, swipe, and purchase meticulously recorded by the omnipresent eyes of the internet. This trove of information has become the lifeblood of Big Tech, enabling targeted advertising, personalized experiences, and powerful algorithms that predict and influence our behavior. However, governments perceive this data collection as a double-edged sword. While it facilitates crime prevention and intelligence gathering, it also raises concerns about:

- Mass Surveillance: The potential for governments to abuse their access to personal data and erode individual liberties.

- Data Breaches: The vulnerability of vast data ecosystems to hacking and leaks, exposing sensitive information to malicious actors.

- Algorithmic Bias: The possibility of biased algorithms perpetuating discrimination and unfairness in areas like law enforcement and loan approvals.

The Skirmish Lines: Encryption, Data Localization, and Right to be Forgotten

Governments have launched various offensives to protect their citizens' privacy and curb Big Tech's data dominion. Some key battlegrounds include:

- Encryption: Governments seeking backdoors to bypass encryption used by messaging apps and other platforms, sparking fierce debates about security and privacy trade-offs.

- Data Localization: Laws mandating local storage of user data within national borders, giving governments greater control but potentially hindering global businesses.

- Right to be Forgotten: Regulations granting individuals the right to request deletion of their personal data from search engines and online platforms, challenging Big Tech's data retention practices.

The New Frontiers: Blockchain and AI Redefining the Battlefield

Emerging technologies like blockchain and artificial intelligence have the potential to reshape the privacy landscape:

- Blockchain: With its decentralized data storage and tamper-proof nature, blockchain offers an alternative to centralized Big Tech databases, potentially empowering individuals to reclaim control over their data.

- AI: Privacy-preserving AI algorithms are being developed to enable data analysis without compromising individual privacy, potentially offering a solution to the tension between data utilization and citizen protection.

The Uncertain Future: Navigating the Digital Minefield

The outcome of this epic battle for privacy remains uncertain. Governments face the pressure of balancing security with individual rights, while Big Tech must navigate the ethical tightrope of innovation and data responsibility. As new technologies emerge, the landscape will only become more complex.

A Call for Collaborative Defense: Citizens as the Ultimate Weapon

Amidst this clash, one key factor remains constant: the voice of the citizens. We, the data producers, must actively engage in this crucial battle. By demanding transparency, advocating for strong privacy laws, and embracing technologies that empower us, we can become the ultimate defense in this digital minefield.

Remember, our privacy is not a privilege, but a fundamental right. Let us raise our voices, wield our knowledge, and fight for a future where technology serves humanity, not exploits it, where the digital world respects the boundaries of our private lives, and where the echo of our footsteps in the online sand fades, leaving only the whispers of individual freedom.

The battle for privacy is far from over. This chapter is just the beginning of a crucial conversation. Together, we can ensure that technology becomes a tool for empowerment, not a weapon of surveillance, and that the shadows of the digital age become not a place of fear, but a refuge for our most precious possession: our right to be unseen, unheard, and utterly ourselves.

Now, go forth, raise your digital shields, and join the fight for a world where privacy reigns supreme.

Government vs. Big Tech: Battle Scars in the Digital Arena

The fight for privacy in the digital age is a clash of titans, with governments wielding the shield of public safety and Big Tech brandishing the sword of innovation, all while citizens stand in the crossfire. This chapter delves into the trenches of this ongoing war, showcasing key battles that have shaped the landscape and highlighting the impact on our digital lives.

1. Facebook's Cambridge Analytica Scandal: In 2018, it was revealed that the personal data of millions of Facebook users had been improperly accessed and used for targeted political advertising by Cambridge Analytica. This case ignited global outrage, raising concerns about data privacy, political manipulation, and the power of social media giants.

Impact: Stricter data protection laws emerged, like the EU's General Data Protection Regulation (GDPR), giving users more control over their data and imposing hefty fines on companies for privacy breaches. Social media platforms faced increased scrutiny and pressure to be more transparent with data practices.

2. Google's Antitrust Battles: Since 2020, Google has been embroiled in antitrust lawsuits filed by the US Department of Justice and multiple states, alleging the company uses its dominant search engine position to stifle competition and harm consumers. Similar investigations are ongoing in Europe.

Impact: Potential changes to search engine algorithms and how online advertising is conducted could arise. Smaller businesses might benefit from a more level playing field in the online marketplace. Consumers may see more diverse search results and potentially lower prices for online services.

3. YouTube's Content Moderation Conundrum: As a platform brimming with user-generated content, YouTube faces the constant challenge of balancing freedom of expression with content moderation. Governments worldwide have pressured the platform to remove videos deemed extremist, hateful, or harmful.

Impact: Stricter content moderation policies can lead to censorship concerns and the removal of legitimate viewpoints. Balancing free speech with harmful content remains a delicate dance, impacting what users see and how they engage with information online.

4. The Great Firewall of China: China's extensive internet censorship apparatus, popularly known as the Great Firewall, restricts access to foreign websites and social media platforms like Facebook and Google. This raises concerns about government control of information and limits access to diverse perspectives for Chinese citizens.

Impact: Limited access to global information can hinder educational and economic opportunities for individuals within China. It also raises concerns about the role of governments in shaping online discourse and suppressing dissent.

5. The Rise of Data Localization Laws: Several countries, including India and Russia, have implemented data localization laws, requiring technology companies to store user data within their borders. This raises concerns about government access to data and potential barriers to global businesses.

Impact: Data localization can increase costs for companies and potentially hinder innovation. It can also restrict data flow and limit access to international services for users in certain countries.

These are just a few examples of the ongoing battle between governments and Big Tech. Each case has far-reaching consequences, impacting how we access information, engage with online platforms, and interact with the digital world. As citizens, it's crucial to stay informed about these developments, understand their implications, and advocate for policies that protect our privacy and promote a free and open internet.

Remember, the digital battlefield is ever-evolving, and our role in shaping its future is vital. By raising our voices, demanding transparency, and supporting solutions that empower individuals, we can navigate the labyrinthine paths of online privacy and emerge on the other side, not as passive data points, but as informed citizens in control of our digital destinies.

Let us march forward, armed with knowledge and vigilance, towards a future where technology serves humanity, not exploits it, and where our digital footprints fade into the shadows, leaving only the echo of our voices demanding a world where privacy reigns supreme.

A Guide to Anonymity in the Big Tech Era

Navigating the digital landscape dominated by Big Tech giants can feel like traversing a minefield. But fear not, for there are ways to safeguard yourself and claim a semblance of anonymity in this data-hungry ecosystem. Here are a few key tactics:

1. Mind Your Data Footprint:

- Minimize data sharing: Be mindful of what information you share on social media and other platforms. Consider using alternative platforms with stronger privacy policies.

- Regularly review privacy settings: Take control of your privacy settings on all platforms you use. Opt out of data sharing wherever possible and limit the information accessible to others.

- Practice digital minimalism: Reduce your online presence by deleting old accounts and content you no longer use. The less data you have out there, the less vulnerable you are.

2. Embrace Encryption:

- Encrypt your communications: Use encrypted messaging apps like Signal or Telegram for private conversations. Consider encrypting your emails and files as well.

- Use a VPN: Virtual Private Networks anonymize your online activity by masking your IP address and encrypting your internet traffic. Choose reputable VPN providers with strong security practices.

3. Be Browser Smart:

- Use a privacy-focused browser: Switch from mainstream browsers like Chrome or Safari to options like DuckDuckGoGo or Brave, which prioritize user privacy and offer built-in tracking protection.

- Install privacy extensions: Add browser extensions like uBlock Origin and Privacy Badger to block trackers and intrusive ads, further minimizing your data footprint.

4. Seek Alternatives:

- Support smaller, privacy-focused platforms: Explore alternatives to popular Big Tech services. Opt for decentralized search engines like DuckDuckGo and cloud storage solutions like Mega for a more private experience.

- Use open-source software: Open-source software offers greater transparency and often prioritizes user privacy over proprietary tools. Consider open-source alternatives for your daily needs.

5. Stay Informed:

- Follow news and updates on data privacy issues: Arm yourself with knowledge about the latest threats and developments in the fight for online privacy.

- Support organizations advocating for digital rights: Join forces with organizations fighting for stronger data protection laws and user privacy.

Remember, absolute anonymity online is difficult, but taking these steps can significantly reduce your data footprint and make it harder for Big Tech companies to track and exploit your information. By adopting a layered approach and remaining vigilant, you can reclaim some control over your digital life and navigate the online world with a greater sense of privacy and security.

So, raise your digital shields, wield your knowledge as your weapon, and march forward toward a future where you control your own data and own your place in the digital landscape.

CHAPTER 12: TAKING BACK YOUR PRIVACY: A CALL TO ACTION

The battle for privacy is not a passive spectator sport. It's a daily battle fought on the keyboards, in the code, and in the halls of power. In this final chapter, we cast off the cloak of the observer and rise as active participants, armed with knowledge and empowered with actionable steps to reclaim our digital sovereignty.

Empowering Yourself: Daily Hacks for Digital Defense

The first line of defense lies in your own hands. Take these steps to fortify your digital walls:

- Audit your digital footprint: Review your social media accounts, subscriptions, and online presence. Purge unused accounts, remove unnecessary permissions, and tighten privacy settings across all platforms.

- Embrace encrypted communication: Use encrypted messaging apps, email encryption tools, and VPNs to shield your online conversations and activities.

- Browse like a ghost: Opt for privacy-focused browsers like DuckDuckGoGo and Brave, and employ browser extensions like uBlock Origin and Privacy Badger to block trackers and invasive ads.

- Become a password ninja: Ditch easily guessable passwords, embrace password managers, and enable two-factor authentication wherever possible.

- Think before you click: Be wary of phishing scams and suspicious links. Be mindful of what information you share online, and avoid oversharing sensitive data.

Building a Collective Fortress: Joining the Privacy Rebellion

Individual actions are powerful, but collective efforts resonate like thunder. Join the privacy revolution by:

- Supporting privacy-focused organizations: Lend your voice and resources to organizations fighting for stronger data protection laws and advocating for user privacy.

- Demanding ethical technology: Voice your concerns to tech companies, government officials, and elected representatives about privacy-invasive practices and demand ethical data usage.

- Educate and empower others: Share your knowledge with friends, family, and colleagues. Help them understand the importance of online privacy and equip them with tools to protect themselves.

- Vote with your clicks: Choose privacy-friendly alternatives to Big Tech services. Support platforms that prioritize user privacy and respect your data.

- Stay informed: Follow news and updates on data privacy issues, emerging threats, and legislative developments.

Beyond the Battlefield: Cultivating a Privacy Mindset

Remember, privacy is not just about technological tools and legislative battles. It's a mindset, a value woven into the fabric of our digital lives. Cultivate a culture of privacy by:

- Practicing mindful online conduct: Be conscious of what you share and where you share it. Remember, the internet is a permanent archive, and once released, digital whispers can carry far.

- Valuing your data as an asset: Your personal information is valuable, not a commodity to be freely traded.

- Demanding transparency and accountability: Hold tech companies and governments responsible for their

data   practices. Demand   clear
explanations, transparent   policies, and   meaningful
consequences for privacy violations.

A Future Woven with Privacy Threads

The path to reclaiming our online privacy is not easy, but
it is paved with the footsteps of countless digital warriors
who came before us. Remember, every conscious click, every
encrypted message, every voice raised in defense of privacy,
contributes to a future where technology empowers, not
exploits, where our digital shadows fade gracefully, and
where we stand tall, not as data points, but as individuals in
control of our own narrative.

So, raise your banner, digital citizen, and join the fight.
Let the echoes of our collective demand for privacy resonate
through the corridors of power and the silicon valleys. Let us
weave a future where technology serves as a tool for freedom,
not a weapon of control, and where our right to digital self-
determination shines bright in the shadows of the internet.

The battle for privacy is far from over, but within each of
us lies the power to rewrite the narrative. Let us be the
authors of a future where privacy reigns supreme, and where
the whispers of our digital lives fade into the ether, carrying
the echoes of a victory hard-won, but well-deserved.

Go forth, digital warrior, and fight for the future of privacy. The shadows await, but so does the dawn of a new era, where you, too, can become a legend in the fight for the most precious right of all - the right to be unseen, unheard, and utterly yourself.

www.ingramcontent.com/pod-product-compliance
Lightning Source LLC
LaVergne TN
LVHW052101060326
832903LV00060B/2454